# A WHITE PREACHER'S MEMOIR

# THE MONTGOMERY BUS BOYCOTT

# A White Preacher's Memoir

## The Montgomery Bus Boycott

### ROBERT S. GRAETZ

Black Belt Press

MONTGOMERY

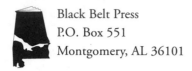
Black Belt Press
P.O. Box 551
Montgomery, AL 36101

Copyright © 1998 by Robert S. Graetz.
All rights reserved under International and Pan-American Copyright Conventions. Published in the United States by the Black Belt Press, a division of Black Belt Publishing, LLC, Montgomery, Alabama.

Originally published as *Montgomery: A White Preacher's Memoir,* Augsburg Fortress, 1991.

Library of Congress Cataloging-in-Publication Data available.

ISBN 1-57966-015-0

Design by Randall Williams
Printed in Canada
99 00 01      5 4 3 2

*The Black Belt, defined by its dark, rich soil, stretches across central Alabama. It was the heart of the cotton belt. It was and is a place of great beauty, of extreme wealth and grinding poverty, of pain and joy. Here we take our stand, listening to the past, looking to the future.*

In loving memory
of our son

ROBERT S. "RAY" GRAETZ III

# CONTENTS

# PREFACE

Jesus asked us to remember him in the sacred Christian celebration of the Lord's Supper. He wants us to remember that he gave his life that we might receive his forgiveness and become his people. If we forget, we risk losing not only our sense of history but also our identity and purpose.

On the human level, there are also men and women who are part of our personal history, those whose actions have had a profound impact on our lives. We are who we are in part because of the contributions they have made. We need to remember them as well. Once again, if we forget, we risk losing not only our sense of history but also our awareness of who we are and why we are here.

It is to some of those people who have had such an impact on our lives that this book is dedicated:

To Mrs. Rosa Parks, Dr. Martin and Mrs. Coretta Scott King, and all the people of color living in Montgomery, Alabama, whose courage and faithfulness made the Montgomery story possible.

To our white friends and supporters in Montgomery, who risked their lives and livelihood, both to demonstrate their love and concern for us and also to convey to their black brothers and sisters that they were not alone in their struggle for freedom and dignity.

To the uncounted numbers of people in the American Lutheran Church, from other faith groups, and from no particular group at all, who kept our spirits buoyed by their prayers, their words of encouragement, and their gifts.

Most of all, to my faithful and loving wife Jeannie, my constant companion, my partner in faith, without whom these memories would have lost much of their richness; and to our seven children, who grew up in the fishbowl atmosphere of a parsonage, learning early that they would rarely have their parents to themselves but would all too often have to share us with the world outside.

I thank them all for the precious memories they have given me to treasure in my heart.

Readers may be disturbed by my frequent use of the terms *"colored"* and *"nigger."* In the 1950s, these terms were frequently used by blacks and whites. I have retained it in order to reflect, as closely as possible, the usage current in the period.

With the dozens of books now on the shelves about the Montgomery movement and Dr. Martin Luther King, Jr., some may wonder why this one should be added. As we read each new book, Jeannie and I realize that we have yet more information to add and a unique perspective to share.

Though there is general agreement that the events in Montgomery marked the beginning of the modern, revitalized, civil rights movement, we do not believe enough attention has been paid to the role of the church or the intervention of God in the Montgomery movement.

Much of the information contained in this book has been verified by the journal of pastoral activities which I maintained while serving at Trinity. My deepest thanks go to that congregation for preserving those records and also making copies available to us.

Thanks also to the Alabama Department of Archives and History and to the Alabama State University for allowing access to newspapers and other artifacts from the time of the Montgomery movement. Without them, some of our memories might not have been refreshed, and this record would not be so complete.

ON JUNE 21, 1991, we lost our oldest son, who was only thirty-seven years old. Bobby, who later called himself Ray, had been a vital part of our Montgomery experience, though he was only a toddler when we arrived. He continued to be a vital part of our lives until his death. Indeed, his presence and his influence have been very much with us through the time since we lost him. We treasure the memories of all the years we shared with him. To our son, and my namesake, this book is lovingly dedicated.

Ray died from AIDS-related illnesses only days before the first edition of *A White Preacher's Memoir* was to be printed. Since then we have had much time to reflect on the significance of his death, and his life. Our family spent many years after our Montgomery experiences working in the civil rights movement. That work still goes on. We have not seen the end of racism, but rather its resurgence in recent years. We humans have a propensity for finding ways of hating and showing disrespect for other people who are not like us.

But in these intervening years we have listened and watched in horror as the vitriol has been spewed forth on others with increasing vehemence, not only on the basis of race, but of gender, religion, language, economic level, one's abilities or disabilities, sexual orientation, or almost any human feature that marks us to be different from one another.

As our ministry has expanded to include all of these groups, we have come to a new awareness of our calling. Just as the disrespect, hatred, discrimination, prejudice, and violence are all of one piece and have a common origin, so our efforts to build bridges, to teach respect, to create peace, and to work toward reconciliation are also of one piece. And they have one source—the love of Jesus Christ, whom we serve.

It is he who called us to our ministry in Montgomery. It is he who yet today enables us to carry on our ministry of love. As we remember the courage of those African-Americans in Montgomery, who sacrificed their own well-being for the sake of generation yet to come, let us pledge ourselves to stand in the face of evil and to reach out with the arms of love to embrace all humankind. As we pass through this world, I pray that our footprints will be marked with love, and that our memories will linger long in the hearts of those we leave behind.

*This is for you, Ray.*

ROBERT S. GRAETZ

# 1

## ANOTHER BOMB!

Startled out of a sound sleep, Jeannie and I sat bolt upright in bed. "My word! Another bomb!" Jeannie cried.

The time was 2:00 A.M. The date, January 10, 1957. The place, the parsonage of Trinity Lutheran Church, 1110 Cleveland Avenue, Montgomery, Alabama. Jeannie had been home from the hospital for not quite four days, having just given birth to our fourth child, a son, David Ellis Graetz. But she was certainly right. It *was* another bomb.

I leaped out of bed and raced through the house, checking the rest of the family. In the next bedroom our two oldest children, Margee—four—and Bobby—almost three—sat up trembling, their wide-eyed faces filled with fear.

"Are you okay?"

"Yes, Daddy. What was that noise?"

"Some bad people bombed our house."

The children were bewildered and frightened but deceptively calm.

Having assured myself that Margee and Bobby were all right, I hurried into the front bedroom. My mother, who had come to help with the new baby, was sharing that room with little Dianne, whose first birthday we would celebrate in just two weeks. Dianne was crying, so I was glad that Mother would be fully occupied.

I ran into the living room and stopped in shock. At the opposite end of the room, the remains of our front door hung at a crazy angle, still partly secured by its hinges. Other pieces of the door were scattered nearby. I could hardly see. The explosion had knocked out our electric

13

power, and a fog of plaster dust hung in the air, obscuring even the glow from the street lights outside. I looked to my left. Where there had been a large picture window overlooking the street, now only a gaping hole remained. Remembering another time our house had been bombed, I glanced down. Fragments of shattered glass covered the entire floor. And there I stood in the middle of it—barefooted!

Suddenly, the face of one of our neighbors appeared in the opening that used to be the doorway. "Everybody all right in there?"

"We're fine, thanks."

Our friend, the manager of the Carver Theatre, a movie house for Negroes in Montgomery, had been visiting some people in the Cleveland Court apartments, about half a block away, when they heard the explosion, the first of six that night in Montgomery.

By the time I put on my robe and went outside, a substantial crowd had gathered in front of our house. Milling around in the darkness, several of us stumbled over a large object in the driveway. Someone produced a match. We leaned over to find out what it was.

If Jeannie had been outside, she could have used her line again: *My word! It was another bomb!* The match, of course, was extinguished immediately, so we didn't get a good look at this new bomb until a few hours later when more light was available. It turned out to be eleven sticks of dynamite taped around a container of TNT, the whole device fastened to what appeared to be part of a television antenna.

The bomb had two fuses. Only one had been lit. Demolitions experts told us later that those fuses were almost totally foolproof. Nothing could have stopped them from working. But our friend from up the street had seen the bomb when he arrived and immediately removed the fuses. We were so thankful he had picked that night to visit with his neighbors into the wee hours of the morning!

The same demolitions people also told us that the bomb should have exploded when it landed, even without the fuses, because of the TNT. They couldn't understand what kept it from blowing up. This was only one of God's many miracles throughout those stressful days.

During the general confusion, someone eventually realized that we should notify the police. Our phone had been knocked out by the blast, but a neighbor offered his. I found the number and dialed, unprepared for the strange conversation that followed.

"Police Department."

"Hello. I'd like to report a bombing."

"Sure, Buddy, tell me all about it. Where is it this time?"

I gave him my address, but he still acted as though he didn't believe me.

Later we discovered why the dispatcher had been so skeptical. The bombers had been clever. Knowing how many police cruisers were on patrol at night, they had phoned in false reports of bombings to distract the cruisers away from the actual sites of their targets. Our house was the first one hit, but already the police department had received more bombing reports than they could handle.

My conversation with the police dispatcher would have been troubling under any circumstances. In the 1950s any contact with a white policeman was unnerving if you happened to be black or associated with black people. The police force represented the front line of the white segregationist army. In earlier times, business and professional men put on their white robes and hoods and rode out as the Ku Klux Klan, using whatever violence and scare tactics were necessary to "keep the niggers in their place." But that kind of illegal activity was no longer tolerated, at least not officially. Nowadays the task of controlling Negroes was entrusted to the legally constituted constabulary. But no matter how much the process was cleaned up, Negroes were still subject to brutal and dehumanizing treatment.

I used to hear stories about people's personal experiences with police all the time. Often the stories dealt with white policemen sexually molesting Negro women. One study of illegitimate babies born to black women in a small Southern city reported that a large percentage of those babies were fathered by white policemen!

So there was always apprehension when it was necessary to call the police. But the Montgomery police arrived soon after we called them, and they took charge of the situation. We were happy to see them remove the bomb, which had been lying in the driveway all that time.

The demolition experts later told us that if the larger bomb had exploded, the entire neighborhood would have been leveled. God was indeed watching over us!

Not until several days later did we realize how traumatic this experience had been for our children.

One night, shortly after putting them to bed, I went into the backyard to take care of our dog. A bad washer on the outside water spigot caused that rumbling, roaring sound that every do-it-yourselfer recognizes. I drew some water for our dog Skippy, unaware of the trauma it caused inside. Our young son started crying and screaming.

Jeannie rushed in to see what was wrong. "What was that noise?" Bobby cried.

"That was just Daddy, getting some water for Skippy."

Though obviously relieved, Bobby still needed to be held for quite some time before he finally calmed down. After a while, Jeannie placed him back in his bed. His eyes had closed, but he was not quite asleep.

As Jeannie left the bedroom, she heard his barely audible voice. "I thought those bad people boomed our house again, but it was only Daddy getting some water for Skippy." He drifted back to sleep with a contented look on his face, his fading voice repeating, "I thought those bad people boomed our house again, but it was only Daddy getting some water for Skippy."

This was Montgomery, Alabama, in the mid-1950s—"The Cradle of the Confederacy." The War between the States (Southerners didn't use the term *Civil War*) may have ended ninety years before according to the history books but not in the hearts of the people who had been on the losing side. In the 1950s many politicians were elected by shouting "Segregation forever!" and by using "nigger-talk." Confederate flags flew everywhere, including the top of the state capitol building.

This was Montgomery, Alabama; we were outsiders from the North, intruders, a threat to the fabric of Southern society (so we were told). In the minds of some people our most grievous sin was that we were white and that we lived and worked with Negroes. Our critics could never understand why we came.

I had grown up in the city. Born in Clarksburg, West Virginia, I spent most of my early years in Charleston, West Virginia's state capital.

Though a metropolitan center, the city was nestled in a narrow portion of the Kanawha River valley. Few places in town were far from the surrounding hills. Even as a small boy, I spent much of my free time hiking and exploring rock formations and caves. Somewhat introverted as a young teenager, I loved to walk the three short blocks from our house to the nearest wood hill, hike to the peak, find a good climbing tree, and perch on a comfortable branch while I looked out over the valley and meditated.

I was the older of Bob and Mackie Graetz's two children, my sister being about two years younger. In our early years, Suzanne was the more extroverted; nevertheless, she became a chemist, and I became a minister. My dad, a chemical engineer, began as a researcher for a glass plant in Clarksburg and then spent the rest of his career working for the Libbey-Owens-Ford Glass Company. Though my mother held paying jobs from time to time, what I remember most are the many hours she spent as a volunteer—working for the Red Cross, knitting warm hats for American sailors during the second World War, filling in wherever she was needed.

I grew up in a largely segregated society in Charleston, attending all-white public schools. There were black people around, but my only real contacts with blacks were with janitors and others in menial positions. Helen, our cleaning woman, was the one I knew best. Otherwise, Negroes had no significance for me. They weren't important. My attitudes reflected those of most white people in the early 1940s. Negroes, often the butt of jokes, were not considered people of any value.

While in high school, two of my friends and I put together a minstrel show. We entertained youth groups as well as church women's organizations. The women were not impressed with our humor, but neither did they see the impropriety of our making jokes at the expense of an entire racial group. To our shame, we didn't either.

When we talked about discrimination at school, we were referring to the treatment of Jews. In the early 1940s, most colleges had "quotas" to limit the number of Jewish students. We cheered with our Jewish friends who managed to squeeze in under the quotas of their chosen schools and grieved with those who didn't.

In 1946, after World War II, I graduated from high school and enrolled at Capital University. I majored in German, in part so that I would be able to read the old theological books that had been passed on to me from my great-grandfather, another Reverend Robert Graetz. From early childhood I had heard German and I spoke a few words of it.

But a sociology course in my junior year completely changed my plans. Doing research for a term paper on discrimination against Jews in higher education, I discovered to my amazement that black people had been almost totally excluded from many U.S. institutions of higher education. I couldn't believe it! That revelation altered my life and my ministry forever.

Switching my major to social science, I also organized a Race Relations Club on campus and joined the National Association for the Advancement of Colored People. Soon I was actively involved in the Columbus chapter of the NAACP, soliciting memberships on campus. A typical new convert, I was full of zeal to eradicate racial prejudice and discrimination wherever it existed.

Also typically, I was naive and unlearned in the field of race relations. It seemed to me that the best way to understand black people would be to become one of them. So I tried to figure out a way to be accepted as a black, being aware by this time that were many Negroes whose physical characteristics made them appear to be Caucasian.

The solution seemed simple enough. I would transfer to a Negro college and pretend I was a Negro. Many years passed before I understood that I could never be accepted as a Negro, no matter how much I wanted to. A wise black friend explained to me, "You always have the option of walking out. We don't."

Jeannie's background was far different from mine. Raised on a farm near the small town of East Springfield, Pennsylvania, near Lake Erie, where her family had lived since the early 1800s, Jeannie was the second of five daughters born to Marshall and Marian Ellis. Like most farmers, Marshall had hoped for sons to help with the "man's work." Even more importantly, no boys had been born into the current generation of Ellises. An old family name was about to be lost. Marshall and Marian kept trying for their boy, but it was not to be. Marshall said resignedly, "The boys will come." (Did they ever! All five daughters are married now and the Marshall Ellis family has become quite a large clan, with many boys in the succeeding generations.)

Jeannie says that not having boys around in no way hindered the farm work. "We were his boys," she reflects. "We did every kind of work that any farm boy ever did." She even maintained a "trap line," catching fur-bearing animals along the creek that meandered through their farm and selling their hides for cash. Working hard, she saved her money, later paying her own way in college.

Sometimes there were unexpected problems with saving money. When Jeannie was still a small girl, her Dad used to give her a nickel a day to do certain early morning chores. Not wanting to squander her hard-earned cash, she buried a tin can in the dirt of the basement floor. Each day she secretly went to the basement, dug up the can, and deposited the day's earnings. Later on, knowing she had accumulated enough to do something special, Jeannie went down to the basement to count her treasure. To her utter dismay, the nickels had all corroded. She thought her fortune had been wiped out. (Later she cleaned off the corrosion, invested the cash, and found a safer way to store her money.)

Although she was petite, Jeannie's small stature never kept her from tackling any size job. (Our children always enjoyed teasing their mom about her height when, one by one, they passed her up.) When she stretches as high as she can, Jeannie just makes it to five feet.

None of her family was tall. But they had the kind of pride that comes naturally to farm families, and with it, plenty of gumption. Jeannie tells a story about her Grandpa Smith. One evening during World War II, the family was gathered in their living room, discussing current events on the battle fields. Grandpa Smith spoke of an action in "Tunsia." Jeannie smiled at him and said innocently, "Grandpa, you mean Tunisia." At that, Grandpa Smith drew himself up to his full five-foot-two height, held his chest out and his chin up, and replied sternly, "I said Tunsia!" When anybody in our family is acting inordinately stubborn, someone else is likely to break the impasse by saying, "I said Tunsia!"

But one particular feature in Jeannie's personality made her a perfect coworker in the ministry we would later share. As a young child, she remembers being attracted to people who were different, even making a point of striking up a conversation with a person who was being ignored by the rest of the group. Those who suffered handicaps or were different from others had a friend in Jeannie Ellis.

When I asked what compelled her to relate to other people in that manner, she cited three factors:

First, it was her way of rebelling against an adult world that didn't live up to her expectations or to their own claims. She couldn't change everyone else, but at least she could do something positive that would help to balance out the unfairness she saw around her.

Second, Jeannie was intrigued by people who didn't live in East Springfield and who didn't look like her. She loved to read about people in other lands.

Third, knowing how Jesus treated people, she says she had a "sporadic Christian zeal" to do the same. That "zeal" has been evident throughout her life, not very sporadic. Jeannie works as hard for Jesus as she did for her dad.

Because of her background, when she was entering her sophomore year at Capital University in Columbus, Ohio, and a blind student needed a roommate, naturally Jeannie was selected. Becoming more than a roommate and a companion to Georgia Griffith, Jeannie learned Braille and spent many hours helping Georgia with her classes (all the while still working to pay her school bills). The relationship between Jeannie and Georgia continues strong to this day. So it was logical that Bob Graetz and Jeannie Ellis would not only join together as husband and wife but that we would end up in Montgomery, Alabama, a white pastor and his wife from the North serving a Negro congregation in the South in the middle of a totally segregated society—so totally segregated that every time we conducted a worship service or had church members in our home, we were violating the law.

Maybe those critics were right. Perhaps we were intruders and a threat to the fabric of their society. But we had not come to Montgomery on our own. We were here because God had brought us here and our story is really the story of God at work in the world and in our lives.

# 2

## MONTGOMERY, 1955

The mid-June trip from Columbus, Ohio, to Montgomery, Alabama, had been long and tiring. The air seemed to grow hotter with every mile we drove. Northerners we were, not used to this steaming southern climate.

Traveling with small children didn't make it any easier. Margee was just over two and a half, and Bobby was fifteen months old. Jeannie was pregnant with our third child, adding to her discomfort during the long, weary hours.

I had been called to serve as pastor of Trinity Lutheran Church, my first charge since being ordained. My ordination ceremony had taken place just the Sunday before, June 12, at my home congregation, St. Paul's Lutheran Church, in Charleston, West Virginia.

In its fifty-three year history, I was the first member of the congregation to enter the ordained ministry. I had invited to preach the sermon that day by a beloved seminary professor, Dr. Herbert Leupold, under whom I studied Hebrew and Old Testament.

Dr. Leupold had imprinted my life. In the classroom where he taught us the Holy Scriptures he encouraged an attitude of holiness. Entering his room, we knew we were walking on holy ground. Even today, when I preach on an Old Testament passage, I find myself sharing some rich image that dear saint of God planted in my mind.

Many family members and old friends came to St. Paul's to help us celebrate. The local television station produced a live program that weekend about my ordination. For me the highlight of the program was a filmed interview with my grandfather, William H. Graetz, who had inspired me to enter the ministry.

In the midst of the joyous festivities, Jeannie and I were under a bit of a strain. Every female relative in my family explained to Jeannie why she shouldn't have any more babies, at least for a while. We already had two children. And Jeannie's first pregnancy had ended when she lost the baby after about three months. She had also had a tubal pregnancy. (The doctor assured us that we would have a difficult time conceiving any more children, since she had only one tube left.) "So," my aunts told Jeannie, "you have to be more careful. It's mostly your responsibility." We didn't tell anyone that we were already expecting another baby.

On that hot June day in the car, we were not thinking about the ordination. By this time we were inside the city limits of Montgomery. With much needed help from friendly service station attendants, we finally made our way to Cleveland Avenue and began watching for our address. Soon we were driving by Trinity Lutheran Church. On the house next to it we saw the number 1110, our address for the next three years.

Into the driveway we turned, weary but relieved, excited but apprehensive. We had arrived in Montgomery, but it was late in the day. And our furniture was not here. Now what were we to do?

At least we could get out of the car and look around. The church building was located on the corner of Cleveland Avenue and Mill Street, where Cleveland began sloping downward. The walkway leading to the church door was almost level with the sidewalk, but by the time the street passed the parsonage next door, the dirt bank at the front of the lot was at least four feet high. Our driveway ascended steeply, then leveled off by the house. Though the pavement ended there, it was possible to continue driving on the dirt, still climbing slightly, into the large open field in back then around the church and out onto Mill Street.

We were not alone for long. Our Ohio license plates and white faces alerted the neighborhood that the new pastor had arrived.

Only later did we discover that there was always someone watching through the windows of homes in Negro neighborhoods, not only out of curiosity but, more importantly, for self-preservation.

*Recent photo of Trinity Lutheran Church, 1104 Rosa Parks Boulevard (formerly Cleveland Avenue), Montgomery, Alabama.*

The Negro in the 1950s lived in a culture where white people had total control over virtually every facet of life. Except for a few black professional and business people serving a Negro clientele, black people's income depended on staying in the good graces of white people.

Whites determined the quality and content of public education, as well as the condition of school buildings. Negroes were relegated to the hardest and most dangerous jobs at the lowest pay. The laws under which both blacks and whites lived were written by white people. (Only a handful of carefully picked Negroes were even allowed to vote at that time.) Life, health, job, and well-being were always at risk, because one could never know when some white person might decide to take out his personal frustrations or prove his sexuality at the expense of the most vulnerable person available—a Negro!

White people in uniform frequently came into Negro sections—mail carriers, milkmen, policemen. During daylight, it was not unusual to see a white person making a delivery or carrying on some other business. But any white people around after dark stirred up anxieties.

It was not uncommon in those days for a white man to have his legal white wife and children at home but to have a Negro family as well. That practice had begun in the slave days and still continued. A candidate for the governorship of Alabama was once asked by a heckler, "What are you going to do about that colored wife and those colored children of yours?"

The politician thought for a moment, then responded, "I'm going to feed them. I'm going to clothe them. I'm going to make sure they have a decent home. What are you going to do about yours?" He was elected! Though the Negro community did not like such arrangements, they reluctantly tolerated them. But they had no intentions of tolerating white men who came into their neighborhoods to force their attentions on Negro women who happened to be on the street or to beat up a Negro man "just for the hell of it."

So they watched, not only for their own sakes, but to protect their neighbors and friends. And they knew everything that went on in their neighborhoods.

We were certainly observed when we pulled into the driveway at 1110 Cleveland Avenue. And it wasn't long before members of Trinity Lutheran Church began arriving at the parsonage. Among the first was a Mr. Robert Dandridge, one of the oldest members of the congregation and one of the most courageous (as we would discover later).

"Welcome to Montgomery," Mr. Dandridge greeted us. "We're glad to see you."

Our members brought more than their words of greeting. Suspecting that we would arrive before the moving van, they had arranged for some temporary furniture, such as mattresses and chairs. They also brought us food to eat.

What warm, wonderful people they were. From the first moment, they let us know that we belonged. That night, as we rested on our borrowed mattresses in a nearly empty house in a city where we had never been before, we knew that we were home.

One of our early memories of those first days in Montgomery was the heat, especially when we were trying to sleep. Only an attic exhaust fan in the hallway provided air circulation for the entire house. Needless to say, the fan was on all night that first night and many other times after that.

Members of Trinity invited us to stay with them. But since we had no idea when our household goods would arrive, we felt we had to remain where we were.

The first morning we awoke about 6:00, hearing a voice calling from somewhere outside, a voice unintelligible to us when it first seeped into our consciousness. Then we caught the words.

"Fresh peas! Get your fresh peas!"

Looking out the picture window that filled a substantial part of the front wall in the living room, we saw an amazing sight. A Negro woman was walking up our street with a large burlap sack balanced on her head. Now this was a touch of home! Jeannie had grown up on a farm, and I had fond memories of working in the little garden in the backyard of my home. We both loved fresh vegetables, especially peas.

Before the woman could get away, we had pulled on our clothes and rushed out to buy some fresh peas. But what a shock! Neither of us recognized what we had purchased. We learned later that they were black-eyed peas. If you wanted the kind we were used to, you had to ask for English peas. But those "fresh peas" were delicious. During our time in Montgomery, we acquired a taste for many wonderful Southern dishes.

When our furniture finally caught up with us, we weren't sure we would be able to keep it. As soon as the truck arrived, the driver asked us to pay for the shipment. Obviously, there had been a mix-up. Since Trinity Church was on mission status, our district office was loaning the congregation enough money to pay for our move. A letter had been sent to the moving company, guaranteeing payment. Because the driver had not been informed of this arrangement, he feared that if he unloaded our furniture without his money, he could end up paying the bill himself. Nothing we said could change his mind.

We had to call Columbus to get this mess straightened out. But that was another problem. During the months that the church had no pastor, the congregation had rented the parsonage, not only for the income but also to prevent vandalism. Though the renters had moved out, they had not paid their phone bill. So we were not allowed to make long distance calls. Calling collect would solve that problem.

I dialed the operator, gave her the number of the Ohio District, and told her I wanted to make a collect call to Dr. Otto Ebert, our district president. In the meantime, Dr. Ebert had already heard about the furniture-delivery confusion. Apparently, there had been some conversations, obviously not too pleasant, between him and the moving company's Columbus office. When our call went through, Dr. Ebert was fuming.

The operator said sweetly, "This is a collect call. Will you accept the charges?"

"Listen, young lady," Dr. Ebert stormed, "we wrote you a letter guaranteeing payment. I've talked to someone there already, reminding them. Get that furniture unloaded!"

"Pardon," said the startled operator. Then she began again, trying to get the answer she had to have before she could get out of the situation. "This is a collect call. Will you accept the charges?"

Before Dr. Ebert could start in once more, I interrupted and explained what was going on. A phone call from him to the moving company and another from the company to our driver, finally liberated our furniture.

Now we really were home. And we could direct our attention to other tasks. Our children were too small to play outside alone. So one of our first purchases in Montgomery was fencing material to enclose the backyard. When the children were a little older, they roamed through the field in back, which must have seemed enormous to them. The center of our block was open, covering perhaps two or three acres. With a fenced-in backyard, we could also have a dog, though a few months passed before Skippy, a lovable mutt from the local dog pound, came to live with us.

Skippy taught us something about Southern life that we wouldn't have believed if we had not witnessed it. From the near corner of the backyard, he could watch people walk up our driveway to the house. And he had a clear view of anyone crossing the back field as well, which was the path many of our members used when they came to see us. We were pleased to hear Skippy bark when people approached.

"He'll be a good watchdog," we told each other. "We got a bonus here."

Then we noticed something strange happening. When the white mailman, the white milkman, or any other white person came to the door, Skippy didn't bark. He wagged his tail and didn't make a sound. At first I thought we were going to have to trade him in for a proper dog for our part of town. Before long, however, Skippy adjusted. His responses reversed. He wagged at our members and barked at the mailman. Somehow even dogs reflected the tension between the racial groups.

In addition to erecting a fence and acquiring a dog, Jeannie and I eagerly looked forward to starting a garden. We had not had a garden since the first summer we were married, four years earlier. I began spading an L-shaped plot, starting behind the fence in back, and continuing down the slope between the house and the church. We noticed that other people's gardens, including that of Mr. and Mrs. B. T. Knox, our next-door neighbors, had deep furrows between the rows of plants. But we were experienced gardeners and "knew" that wasn't necessary.

Mr. Dandridge, who used to drop by frequently, sometimes every day, wondered out loud if I would be able to spade that whole plot. It *was* a good-sized garden we had planned. He suggested getting someone to plow the ground. Then it would be done right without all the hard work on our part.

Mr. Dandridge knew just the man for the job. Before long a stranger showed up in back of the house with a mule and a hand-guided plow. We watched as he directed the mule back and forth, turning over the sod, making those deep furrows we had seen. Later that day Mr. Dandridge came by to inspect the man's work, which, he declared, was not up to the proper standards for his pastor. Because the man had charged us such a small amount for his work, we were surprised when Mr. Dandridge told us we hadn't gotten our money's worth. In those days Negroes' wages were so low that people who did odd jobs never thought to ask for much. The few times we hired someone to do a job for us, we had to argue with them to convince them to accept more money. Even then we felt guilty about how little we paid. But Mr. Dandridge promised us that something would be done about this bad plowing job. Sure enough, the next day the man and his mule came back.

Soon afterward, however, we leveled the ground so we could plant a "proper" garden. Then we made our own rows and planted our seed. Later, seeing what we had done, Mr. Dandridge raised some questions about our flat garden on the sloping ground, but he didn't try to stop us. I think he decided we had to learn for ourselves.

Our first big rain arrived after some of the seeds were already germinating. Following the storm we found a collection of seeds and sprouts piled at the bottom of our garden. We were grateful for the long growing season in Alabama. There was still time to replant. And this time we had deep, deep furrows.

The following spring, we bought a combination hand plow and cultivator. Though we discovered that the plow wasn't much use in that thick sod, we used the cultivator for many years.

The gardening and fence-building, however, had to fit into the time available along with our other responsibilities. We had come to serve, and there was much to do.

Jim and Jean Darnell, dear friends of ours, had come to Alabama the same time we did. Jim and I graduated from the seminary together. He had received a call to St. Paul's Lutheran Church in Birmingham, about one hundred miles north of Montgomery. The first two Sundays we were in Alabama, Dr. Ebert preached and installed the two of us as pastors in our respective congregations, me in Montgomery on June 26 and Jim in Birmingham on July 3.

The time in between the two installation services had been set aside as a week of Bible camp for the Alabama Conference—about six active congregations and a few small preaching stations.

From the moment we arrived Jim and I learned a great deal about Southern customs. At the campground near Tuscaloosa, Alabama, one small dormitory housed the children and counselors, but we could not stay there. Jim and I, as well as the other two white participants, District President Otto Ebert and another church official, stayed in a tent erected for us next to the left field foul line on the ball diamond. The Negro pastors were willing to risk having us involved in illegal interracial activities during the day, but they feared the repercussions if anyone found out we were sharing their sleeping facilities.

We rather enjoyed the arrangement. All four of us loved camping, so the tent didn't bother us. And we were free from all responsibilities for shepherding the boys and girls after nightfall. Each evening the four of us got into a car and headed for a dairy store in Tuscaloosa. There we sat and ate ice cream and visited until bedtime. Jim and I really enjoyed getting to know our district president personally. He was a great friend and became a strong supporter for Jeannie and me when things got difficult later on.

Jim and I also created a scandal during the Bible camp. The swimming pool was located next to a small back road. Each afternoon during the campers' swim time, Jim and I never missed a chance to get into the water. Not used to the heat, we needed the swim just to cool off.

By the second or third day we noticed considerably more traffic on that little road, drivers moving slowly by, their eyes glued to the scene at the swimming pool. I suppose they couldn't believe that white people would swim with Negroes. Jim and I thought it was a great joke. Neither the other pastors nor the children said anything about it, but later we realized that we could have ended up in jail, or worse, besides creating serious problems for the rest of our group.

Jeannie and I visited with the Darnells quite often, usually at their house or ours. Our friendship at the seminary had grown strong as we ministered to them when their firstborn baby died. We remembered too well losing our own first child, long before it was due to be born.

By the time we arrived in Alabama, the Darnells had a son, Tim, about the same age as our children, and they were expecting their second child.

Another force that drew us together was our common status, both white Northerners serving Negro congregations in the South, both "intruders," both suspect.

Our living arrangements were more comfortable than the Darnells. Our house was new, theirs only newly painted. We'll never forget our tour of their house on our first visit. Whoever did the painting was certainly thorough. Nothing had been missed—light switches, ceiling fixtures, woodwork. They used the same color throughout the house, an unusual shade of yellowish gold. In each room, everything visible was painted that same color.

Neither we nor the Darnells had an easy time adjusting to the Southern way of life. It seemed that just about everything we did in those days was either illegal or contrary to Southern customs. Myriad state and local laws mandated segregation in every aspect of life, not always enforced but always there if needed.

We tried never to knowingly use any segregated facility or business. That included the white-patronized theaters downtown, where Negroes were allowed to sit only in a segregated balcony. Once in a great while, there would be a good picture showing at the Carver Theatre, a Negro cinema. But the manager dared not let us buy tickets for fear of being arrested. Anytime we wanted to see a movie, he would let us in free.

Getting a haircut was another problem. Not wanting to cause a problem for any of the Negro barbers, I started going to a nearby white barber shop. At first this arrangement worked fine, but after my involvement in the bus boycott, no one would speak *to* me; everyone spoke *at* me. The moment I walked in the door, the conversations changed from weather and sports to "nigger talk."

Soon, the owner of the shop was the only one who could cut my hair. No matter how full the shop was, when my turn came, the other barbers would say, "I'm going to step outside for a minute" or "I'm going to take a break." As soon as the owner was free and I was in his chair, the others returned.

I also became more and more nervous about having that barber shave my neck with his straight razor, knowing how he felt about me. I finally told Jeannie, "I'm not going back there anymore. I'm going to a Negro barber."

This solved *my* problems, but caused worse problems for the unfortunate barber I chose. First, he was so nervous it took him much longer to cut my hair. Second, if a white salesman came in while I was in the chair, that poor, frightened barber danced around me to keep the salesman from seeing who was sitting there.

So I gave up and appealed to Jeannie. "You've been cutting Bobby's hair. Could you start cutting mine as well?" She's been my barber ever since.

Other problems surfaced in the area of yard work. When we arrived in Montgomery, our front yard needed attention. Though it had been graded the same time the house was built, not much had been done to it since. Morning person that I am, I went out early several times a week trying to get the lawn in shape.

Once again, I discovered I wasn't acting like a proper Southerner. Normal, decent white people were not supposed to do yard work. A yard "boy" would work for two or three dollars a day, so almost every family could afford to hire someone to do the "nigger work." Many near accidents occurred in front of our house as men driving to work in the morning would gawk at me in my old clothes, working on the lawn. On that high bank in front of the house, my white face was all too visible.

One of our most pleasant memories of that front yard was the fig tree right in the center. Not only had we never seen a fig tree, but we had never tasted fresh figs. After the first taste, we were hooked. But in a few weeks we discovered we had been devouring unripe figs. They got even better with time.

But the front yard created another problem. Since our congregation was always short of money, the men took turns cutting the grass around the church building while I kept the parsonage lawn mowed. But our schedules rarely coincided. Because the grass grew extremely fast in that hot climate, one side of the expansive lawn in front of the two buildings was usually several inches higher than the other. We resolved that by making a list of volunteer mowers, including me, and took turns mowing both lawns. That arrangement worked well most of the time. But once in a while a volunteer would forget his turn, or his mower would be out of commission. The grass grew so fast that even one missed weekly turn left a jungle out front.

Jeannie would suggest rather strongly that I go ahead and cut the grass, but I have always felt I should not take over other people's responsibilities. Instead, I would get out the lawn mower and cut a path from our front door to the door of the church. Generally, that was all it took.

Others would see the path and make sure the errant volunteer got there quickly to do his job.

Part of the problem was that we had an old-style push mower. The others had motorized versions. When theirs weren't running, they didn't want to borrow ours. Before long, they took to borrowing each other's mowers to avoid seeing my little path.

The people at Trinity were proud of their church and wanted the place to look good. They took pride in their denomination also. Though Lutherans constituted only a small percentage of the population in the South, white or Negro, some of the families in our congregation had been Lutherans for generations. Trinity Lutheran Church had been founded in 1915, during a period when several Lutheran congregations were established in Negro communities in Alabama and Mississippi.

But even those weren't the first. In an updated pamphlet called "Lutheran Work in Interracial Communities" (published by the Division of American Missions of the former National Lutheran Church), Pastor Ervin E. Krebs wrote about the beginnings of Lutheran work in Negro areas.

Admitting that the Lutheran Church had not made a major effort to establish congregations in Negro communities, he noted that some work had begun as early as 1666 in black and interracial communities in what was then the Danish West Indies, later called the Virgin Islands.

He described the work of the Synodical Conference in the South, beginning in 1877; the start of a congregation in Washington, D.C., in 1885, among immigrants from the Virgin Islands; and another in Baltimore in 1890.

Early in this century, the former American Lutheran Church began developing congregations and Christian day schools in Alabama and Mississippi, including Trinity Lutheran Church, Montgomery.

Those Christian day schools were extremely important. Public schools for Negro children were poor at best. As late as 1955, when we reached Montgomery, we heard horror stories about what passed for education in Negro communities.

One of our members was principal of a rural school north of Montgomery. Attendance was sparse in the fall because the children were kept at home to pick cotton. Those additional hands made the difference between the family making it or going under. In the spring, children again missed school in large numbers, so they could "chop cotton," hoe the weeds in the cotton patch. Teachers were forced to mark the children present to avoid losing state funds based on average daily attendance. State officials knew what was going on, but they ignored it.

In the 1950s, Lutheran missions in Negro communities were looked upon as much the same as foreign mission fields. When Jim Darnell and I accepted our calls to Alabama, not a single student in our class was going into foreign work. Our commitment, however, eased the consciences of our classmates. "We don't have any foreign missionaries," they would say, "but at least we have you two."

Furthermore, since we ourselves were an immigrant church, we had very few Negro pastors to serve in those communities. The American Lutheran Church reflected its German heritage. Many of its churches still conducted services in German. When Lutheran churches had been established in Alabama and Mississippi, white German pastors had gone south to serve them.

Though the War between the States had been over for fifty years or so, the early part of the twentieth century was still a dangerous time for white people to work with Negroes in the South. Courageous people risked their lives to share the Gospel of Jesus Christ with their brothers and sisters of color.

Some white people had come south to establish educational programs for Negroes. Since schools for "colored" people threatened the whites' way of life even more than churches did, educators found their lives in greater jeopardy. Older people told us about such teachers being moved from house to house at night to prevent the Ku Klux Klan from finding and harming them.

In the early 1950s the situation improved markedly. Southern white leaders bragged about the fine schools they provided for Negro children. Obviously, however, the improvements came largely after legal pressures, including the 1954 U.S. Supreme Court decision declaring segregated public schools unconstitutional. Those court decisions threatened the South's basic "separate-but-equal" principle, their generations-old belief that their Negroes were just as well off as white people.

When we first arrived in Montgomery, white people were more curious than belligerent; many Negroes were downright suspicious.

One Sunday morning, Mr. Lonnie Wagstaff, a long-time Trinity member, walked into our church laughing. As he had walked down the street, he saw some men lounging in front of the tavern across from Trinity. Recognizing him as one of our members, one of the men said loudly to his fellow loungers, "I don't need no white man to teach me how to live."

Inside the church Mr. Wagstaff shook his head sadly. "They're just ignorant," he told me.

Members of Trinity had no trouble adapting to a white pastor. They had been served by white pastors before. We just happened to be the first to live next to the church.

But the offensive realities of racial segregation reached even into the field of medicine. Because our new baby was due in January of 1956, we needed to find an obstetrician for Jeannie soon after our arrival. Hospital facilities were strictly segregated, so we needed to secure a white doctor. (For routine medical matters, we patronized Negro doctors.)

Before leaving Columbus, we had asked our doctor there to refer us to a Montgomery obstetrician, but the best he could do was to give us a name out of a directory. After arriving in Montgomery, we discovered that the recommended doctor was known to accept Negro patients as well as white. So we went to him.

The Negro patients, however, had their own waiting room, so there was no contact between the two groups of patients. That probably would have been the case wherever we would have gone, given the legal situation.

Jeannie's doctor was nice enough, though he didn't say much and didn't agree with what we were doing. But after his office nurse found out that we were living in a Negro neighborhood and working in a Negro church, she became almost hostile. Every time Jeannie came into the office, this nurse lectured her about the impropriety of what we were doing. And she seemed unnecessarily rough and careless in her preliminary examinations of Jeannie.

In spite of the nurse, Jeannie felt comfortable enough with the doctor to continue with him through Dianne's birth and also through her next pregnancy. That doctor showed his true mettle when our house was bombed the second time (January 1957), just after David was born. Within hours of the bombing, while crowds of people were milling around and reporters were carefully noting who was coming and going, our doctor came bursting into the house. "Where's my patient?" he shouted. He didn't care who saw him there. He was just being a good doctor.

After Dianne was born on January 24, 1956, we were referred to a friendly, helpful white pediatrician. And when Jeannie became pregnant with Kathy at the end of 1957, we found another obstetrician, who was not only very nice to us but also supported our efforts.

Jeannie had some misgivings about her new doctor when she found out that all of the doctors in his group practice would be working with her during her pregnancy. When she asked how the others would respond to her, the doctor assured here, "Well, I'm a Jew, and they're in practice with me. That should tell you how open-minded they are."

We had a surprising number of white friends, including many Jews, in Montgomery. A reporter from The *Montgomery Advertiser* said to me one day, "My publisher wants me to ask you what it's like being part of the pariah."

"What's that?" I asked. I had never heard the word.

"A social outcast," he explained.

"Oh," I said, "I don't know what it's like. We have friends all over town, white and Negro."

We had discovered quite early that there was an underground network of so-called "liberals" who maintained close contact with each other. Soon after we arrived, some of them began inviting us to their homes, introducing us to new friends. Even after our bus boycott involvement endangered those who befriended us, they never turned their backs. They willingly jeopardized their own safety to preserve our friendship. A number of such friends stand out in our memories.

Mr. and Mrs. I. B. Rutledge, an older couple, were both members of established Southern families. Mrs. Clara Rutledge, a proper Southern lady, rather mothered Jeannie. She found out about us not long after we arrived in Montgomery and invited Jeannie to a luncheon with like-minded women. She encouraged Jeannie's involvement with other women's groups as well, such as the Women's International League for Peace and Freedom (WILPF), a group focused on building better human relationships.

While white *men* were shouting "Segregation forever!" and working hard to preserve their cherished traditions, white *women* all over the South were working just as hard to eliminate racial prejudice and segregation. Some were quite outspoken. Mrs. Rutledge was one of the finest, a remarkable, fearless woman, who lived into her nineties.

Through Mrs. Rutledge, Jeannie met Jane Katz, and we later became acquainted with her husband, Warren. About our age, the Katzes had young children, were very concerned about social issues, and shared many of our deeply held values. For Warren, a local businessman, even to admit that he knew us was an act of courage. But Warren and Jane not only knew us, they were among our best friends. Though Jewish, they were more accepting of us than many Christians we knew.

Jeannie and Jane spent a great deal of time together. They went through pregnancies together, walked their children together, and in one of the rare breaches of our no-segregated-facilities policy, they took the children to a whites-only wading pool together. Jeannie felt guilty every time they went because her Negro friends couldn't go along. Not only could they not go to the white park, there was no comparable pool for Negroes. But this policy breach was probably an important tension release when the pressure on us was the greatest.

The Katzes often invited us to their house for dinner parties, but I soon learned that their friends did not all share our values. At one of the parties I became engaged in a heated discussion about segregation and desegregation. Jane maneuvered me away from the group. "Just because people come to our house doesn't mean they think like we do," she warned. After that I was more careful about what I said to their guests.

We enjoyed another kind of party each year, a greens-gathering party at Morrison and Vivian Williams's farm, a few miles outside of Montgomery. What fun we had! Most of our close white friends were there, including Morry's parents, Aubrey and Anita Williams. Morry would load us all onto a farm wagon and pull us with his tractor back into the woods to find Christmas trees, holly, mistletoe, and greens for decorating. Even the little children took part. We had a day-long party, hidden away from the concerns of church, boycott, violence, anything. Truly a wonderful escape!

Warren and Jane Katz, though Jews, seemed to have as much fun gathering Christmas decorations as the rest of us. They were not alone. Victor and Anne Kerns, another young Jewish couple with children about the same ages as ours, were also part of that group. They too were generous about inviting us to their home. We felt blessed that our children could grow up with friends who were both Negro and white, Jew and Christian.

Clifford and Virginia Durr helped us escape from time to time to a piece of rural land they owned outside of Wetumpka, a few miles from Montgomery. They called it the Pea Level. We never asked where the name came from. I always assumed they used to grow black-eyed peas there. Cliff and Virginia had a nice home in Montgomery where we were frequent guests, but they were also building a cottage at the Pea Level as a retirement home. Cliff, an attorney formerly involved in the Franklin Roosevelt administration, now practiced law in Montgomery, but he had lost considerable business due to his support of Negro rights. During the Montgomery bus boycott, Cliff was one of the few whites who openly worked with Negro attorneys, defending the boycotters.

Jeannie and I enjoyed taking our children out to the Pea Level, partly to visit with the Durrs, and partly to get some exercise, helping them build their house. Maybe they were an inspiration for us. More than twenty years later, we helped build our own home on a hilltop in rural southeastern Ohio, where we now live.

Virginia Durr also inspired and encouraged us through her autobiography, entitled *Outside the Magic Circle*.

We *were* outsiders, of course. We were also intruders. And we *did* threaten the societal fabric of the time. We knew that. But plenty of people around us, Negro and white, reinforced our conviction that the fabric not only needed to be changed but to be torn apart. And they were willing to stand with us as we allowed God to use us in that process. Even in the worst of times we knew we were never alone. God was always present, not only in his Spirit but also in his people.

*Bob and Jeannie Graetz, June 10, 1951.*

# 3

## TRINITY'S NEW PASTOR

After my race-relations "conversion" as a sociology student at Capital University in the fall of 1948, my entire life focus changed. Growing up, I was the skinny kid everybody picked on, so I deeply empathized with underdogs and outcasts.

By the time I reached high school, I had developed a brash assertiveness, which masked and later supplanted my negative self-image. My consistent good grades in school became my comfort. If I couldn't be superior in physical activities, at least I had *something* I could do better than most people.

But before college I had never given any serious thought to Negroes or to my relationship with them. My research on discrimination in higher education had brought me my first face-to-face exposure to the realities of racial segregation. I hated what I had seen. I had to do something about it—if only to preserve my own integrity.

Up to that point, I had been playing at going to college. Few of my courses presented much of a challenge. But my new awareness of the plight of America's Negroes generated a new, much more serious attitude toward my studies.

I also became more and more involved in the Negro community of Columbus and in human relations activities on campus.

In the meantime, Jeannie Ellis had become part of my life. Early in my senior year, I kept noticing a freshman who headed for Lehman Hall to check her mailbox each day about the same time as I was going the opposite direction to my Greek class in the library basement. Her shy smile and sparkling eyes captivated me.

It was not until February 12 that we had our first date. I asked Jeannie to go with me to the Luther League retreat at an old mansion about a mile from the campus. She wrote in her diary that she wished she had been asked by a different young man, one whom she had secretly admired.

The day of the picnic was dreary and rainy, but we didn't mind. We spent virtually the entire day perched on a window seat, unmindful of the crowds around us, sharing ourselves with each other, learning that we had many values and interests in common. By late afternoon our lives were permanently and totally bound together. We walked the mile back to the campus in the rain, hand in hand, passing up all offers of rides from others at the retreat. Upon our return, Jeannie told one of her roommates, "Whoever marries Bob Graetz will sure be lucky," and I knew in my heart that Jeannie Ellis would one day be my wife.

From that moment on we were inseparable. One of my clergy colleagues claims he remembers my running late into class, having rushed out during the break to walk Jeannie to her next class.

We were engaged the following summer, and one year later, on June 10, 1951, Jeannie and I were married in her home congregation, the Federated Church of East Springfield.

The Evangelical Lutheran Theological Seminary was just across the street from Capital University. So Jeannie was able to continue her studies in elementary education at Capital during the year we were engaged, and she took a few courses the first year we were married. By that time, however, Jeannie was working full time, primarily to help put me through seminary. So her formal education was interrupted for about ten or fifteen years.

During my seminary years, we became involved with St. Philips Lutheran on the east side of Columbus, a totally Negro congregation, except for the white pastor and his family.

At that time of our first contact, the church was located on the west side of town but had purchased a lot on East Long Street. In the fall of 1950, Pastor Edward Keim came out to Capital to recruit some student volunteers. A gift load of paving bricks had been dumped on the church's lot and needed to be stacked out of the way of the construction crew expected the following week. Jeannie and I volunteered to help. On a rainy Saturday in October, we had a date—stacking bricks!

After the church building had been erected, we were involved in a wide range of activities at St. Philips, filling in for Sunday school teachers and attending special events, even waiting tables for a church dinner, so the members could all participate. They were honoring two Negro seminary graduates with calls to Alabama—Harvard Stephens to St. Paul's in Birmingham, and Nelson Trout to Trinity in Montgomery. We had no idea that in three years we would be making the same trip. Nor could we have dreamed that in a little more than six years, I would be St. Philips's pastor.

Lutheran seminaries require a year of internship, usually after the second year of academic work, placing each student with an experienced pastor who served as trainer and supervisor. But my assignment was a different type of internship. A lay pastor serving a small, mostly Negro congregation in Los Angeles, California, Community Lutheran Church, was coming to the seminary to prepare for ordination. I was assigned to take his place.

For my on-the-job training, I would be the sole pastor. A neighboring pastor would only check on me from time to time.

Jeannie was carrying our first baby then. The doctor would not allow her to drive with me to California because she had miscarried in her earlier pregnancy. She stayed with her family in Pennsylvania for a few weeks, flying out to join me after I got settled. In August 1952, I loaded our belongings into our 1941 Ford and began the long drive.

Just a year later that car gave up. Driving to a church conference, I stopped to pick up my supervising pastor, but the car wouldn't start again. So the pastor called a mechanic in his congregation and took us in his own car. When we returned after the conference, the mechanic had a message for me. "I've fixed the car so you can drive it home. But don't expect it to go any farther. It's dead!"

Now we had a problem. Our salary of $175 per month met our needs, but barely. There was no room in the budget for a car payment. Meanwhile, word of our crisis had spread. My supervisor sent us to a car dealer who was a member of his congregation. And his Sunday school took up a special offering for us.

As we drove up to the car dealership and saw the sign, Oldsmobile–Cadillac, we almost drove on. We *knew* we couldn't afford anything there. But because I promised to see the salesman, we went in, trying to think of a nice way to tell him he couldn't help us. That man had obviously pulled some strings because he showed us a beautiful Oldsmobile that was far cheaper than any of the Fords, Chevys, or Plymouths of the same year.

But there was still no room in the budget for even a small car payment. To my amazement, I heard myself asking the salesman, "How much time will we have if this is going to be a cash deal?"

"Ninety days," he answered with a puzzled look on his face.

"All right," I said, "write it down as a cash deal. We can't afford the monthly payments."

We signed the papers and walked out. I couldn't believe what I had said.

Soon the check arrived from my supervisor's Sunday school. Then another check came from the pastor who chaired our district mission committee. Money came in from everywhere. My grandfather, who knew nothing about what was going on, wrote us a letter, saying he thought we might be needing a little help, and he enclosed a substantial check. Just before the ninety-day deadline, we added up what we had received. After we deducted our tithe, the ten percent we regularly set aside for the Lord's work, the total came to about $750, the price of our car! Then the checks stopped coming.

That experience taught us a great deal about God's providence and the way he keeps his promises.

My one-year internship stretched into two, and we have always been grateful for the additional experience.

Community Lutheran was the only congregation of any denomination in the middle of that large tract development. Located between Los Angeles and Compton, a southern suburb, it was a typical new community with acres of small houses on small lots, all built according to a handful of floor plans. The entire area had been farmed not long before.

At the edge of our neighborhood was a dairy farm. We bought our milk and ice cream there. It was fun to see the cows so close.

This new development was originally intended for white people, but when we arrived, the community was becoming mostly Negro. Our church was there to receive the newcomers. Membership grew from seventy-five to one hundred and fifty. Sunday school enrollment swelled to over five hundred, overwhelming our little building. Soon we developed three Sunday schools, two of them meeting in our own building during successive hours, and a third in two double garages a few blocks away.

We could never have made it without help. The American Lutheran Church sent us a miracle worker named Thelma Tollefson. A traveling parish worker, she served primarily mission congregations, providing assistance for special programs and helping establish new congregations. She specialized in teaching small children. One summer she led a series of vacation Bible schools as well. Without Thelma, Community Lutheran could never have experienced such remarkable growth.

CALIFORNIA initiated us to racial violence. Just south of the church, two Negro families moved onto a previously all-white block. In spite of considerable vandalism to their houses, they stayed on. The frightful experience of working with families and community leaders to guarantee a peaceful reception for the Negroes provided valuable training for future events. Living in a largely Negro area, we learned to look beyond race or the color of a person's skin.

During our two years at Community Lutheran, we had two children. Margaret Ellen (Margee) was born November 3, 1952, and Robert Sylvester, III (Bobby), on March 13, 1954. In the summer of 1954 we headed back to Columbus. Although the cross-country drive with two small children presented a challenge, we eventually returned to the campus, found an apartment to live in, and prepared for classes again.

Because we had no savings, during my senior year in the seminary I was working full time in addition to my classwork while Jeannie kept busy with the children.

During our Christmas visit with Jeannie's family, she suffered some abdominal pains. After we returned home, the pain grew worse, and she began to bleed. I rushed her to Ohio State's University Hospital.

Leaving Jeannie in the car, I raced into the emergency room. "My wife's pregnant," I shouted, "and she's in the car outside!"

"Is she fullterm?" a nurse asked.

Panicky, I didn't understand what she meant. "Yes," I said.

"Then let's get her in here."

As soon as they saw here, someone asked, "Did she already deliver?"

"No, but she's bleeding!" I cried.

Finally, the emergency-room crew understood, and they admitted her for what we later learned was a tubal pregnancy.

While she was recuperating from surgery, a steady stream of student doctors paraded through her room because University was a teaching hospital. As her doctor explained, "We don't get many ectopic (tubal) pregnancies, so everyone wants to see you."

The doctor also warned us that we would have a difficult time having any more babies because the surgery removed one of Jeannie's tubes. (Years later, we reported to him that she had given birth to four more children after her surgery. Then we secured his services to deliver our seventh child, our last.)

Factors beyond our control necessitated three moves that year. I fell far behind in my school work because I could do little more than attend classes. The understanding seminary professors told me to make up the work whenever I could.

At semester break in January, I took Jeannie and the children back to her home in Pennsylvania, and I moved in with my sister and her husband, Bill Deutschmann, my seminary classmate. For the rest of the school term, I did little more than attend classes, work, complete current and makeup assignments, and write daily notes to Jeannie. Suzanne and Bill rescued us from an impossible situation.

Struggling to survive that difficult year, Jeannie and I sensed that God might be preparing us for something even more difficult. We talked about it frequently, drawing strength to hold on until the end of the school year. During that last semester, Jeannie and I were together for only one day, Easter Sunday.

Also during that semester, senior seminarians were assigned to districts. Dr. Otto Ebert, the Ohio district president, had asked for me. He knew of my work in California, and Trinity Lutheran Church, in Montgomery, Alabama, needed a pastor. Its former pastor, Nelson Trout (who eventually became Bishop of the A.L.C.'s South Pacific District) had been called to serve at my former internship post, Community Lutheran Church in Los Angeles. Dr. Ebert had given the leaders at Trinity a good report about the senior seminarian who had served his internship in a Los Angeles Negro congregation. Sight unseen, Trinity accepted me and sent a letter of call. And I quickly accepted.

Church officials knew of my zealous race-relations activities as an undergraduate at Capital, and they knew about my peacemaking role after the violence in our California parish. So executives from the district and national offices summoned me for a special meeting in Columbus.

They stressed that my primary tasks were to proclaim the Gospel of Jesus Christ and to serve my people. "The South is not receptive to intruders from the North," they explained. "You will bring harm to yourself and your family, not to mention the congregation and the church at large, if you go to Montgomery crusading for racial justice.

"I am going to Montgomery to be a pastor," I assured them. "I won't start any trouble, I promise."

And, contrary to what many people believe, I kept that promise.

So Trinity Lutheran Church had a new pastor. The *Montgomery Advertiser,* one of our two daily newspapers, carried the story, but more than half of its subscribers never had an opportunity to read it. The *Advertiser* had a Negro edition, a common practice of that period. One page from the regular paper, probably society news or something else relevant only to the white community, was pulled out and replaced with Negro news, largely from churches and social clubs. Whites rarely cared what was happening to "colored" people anyway, except those who worked for them.

As Jeannie and I got to know the members of Trinity, we fell more in love with them every day. And they accepted us totally, in spite of the race difference. In Los Angeles our church had a few members who were not Negro. Not so in Montgomery. There were only four white members in the congregation—Bob Graetz, Jeannie Graetz, Margee Graetz, and Bobby Graetz.

Though there had been white pastors at Trinity before, the Negro community was still suspicious. That suspicion diminished considerably when I participated openly in the bus boycott, but it did not totally disappear until August 1956 when our house was bombed for the first time.

When we arrived, however, we weren't thinking about boycotts or any other such activities. Church work took priority and obligations extended beyond trinity. Some Alabama Negro congregations organized early in the century had disbanded as people moved off the plantations into the city. Others had lost many of their members but still continued to function. Unable to afford full-time pastors, they were maintained as preaching stations. I was responsible for two of those: St. Paul's Lutheran in Clanton, a small town about forty miles north of Montgomery, and rural St. Mark's Lutheran, near Wetumpka in Elmore County, about twenty miles northeast of Montgomery. I had heard that Elmore County was a hotbed of Ku Klux Klan activity, but that didn't worry me until the boycott began.

I led services at Wetumpka in an old school building on the fourth Sunday afternoon of each month. Mr. John Sanders served as lay leader. In fact, his large family made up a substantial portion of the congregation.

But these rural folks had little use for clocks. Sun and daylight determined their timetables. I heard stories about rural people looking outside on a Sunday morning and saying to the family, "The neighbors are heading to church. We'd better get ready."

Driving to the church outside of Wetumpka on Sunday afternoon, I was occasionally the first one there. As others arrived, we would visit for a while. Finally Mr. Sanders would look around and announce, "Looks like most everybody's here. Let's start the service."

Sometimes, when the folks came even later than usual, Mr. Sanders would say to me, "They're a little slow in gathering today." Occasionally they didn't make it at all. One entry in the church journal at Trinity simply says, "Drove to Wetumpka. No service because of heavy rain."

One day I needed to talk with Mr. Sanders, so I drove to his small plantation and found him and his children picking cotton. Since it was the first time I had actually seen this operation up close, I had to try it for myself. The Sanders family willingly obliged. First they showed me how to pull the puffs of cotton out of the sharp, dried bolls that had popped open. Then they slipped over my shoulder a long bag that seemed to drag ten or fifteen feet behind me. Cotton is so light that even a large bagful is not too heavy to drag along. And the larger the bag, the fewer wasted trips to the edge of the field to empty it.

As I walked between two rows, stooped over, picking with both hands, I felt pleased that I was doing just what they showed me. Furthermore, instead of taking Mr. Sanders away from his work, I was helping. Before long, however, it became obvious that something was amiss. The whole Sanders family had stopped working and stood around, laughing at me. I was disrupting their work, not helping. And Mr. Sanders told me that at the rate I was picking, I would make only a dollar or two for a full day's work. I was so slow, I never would have survived as a cotton picker.

The other preaching station, St. Paul's at Clanton, had a worship service every Sunday afternoon. I preached there about twice a month. On the other Sundays, Mr. Daniel Mitchell, a member of Trinity, preached. He was also Trinity's regular delegate to district conventions in Columbus, Ohio. Because Mr. Mitchell worked for the Louisville and Nashville Railroad, he could travel anywhere he wanted for nothing. Trinity couldn't afford to send anyone else, and Mr. Mitchell willingly took the responsibility.

The location of the Clanton church caused some problems that we didn't experience at Wetumpka. Clanton's cinder-block church building in the Negro community stood on a through street. If white people, out for a Sunday afternoon drive, drove past while I was greeting parishioners before or after the service, they were shocked to see my white face and nearly drove off the road.

After the bus boycott started and my involvement became known, the people at Trinity became increasingly concerned about my driving alone through the countryside to these preaching stations. I learned all the back roads to our church outside of Wetumpka, and I was careful to take a different route each time I went to or from Clanton. Though we were not aware of it at the time, I was often followed when I drove outside of Montgomery.

Besides Wetumpka and Clanton, my responsibilities took me regularly to the Veterans' Hospital in Tuskegee and to several other places in Alabama. The church council asked me to have one of the men of the church accompany me when I went out of town. More often than not, Mr. Robert Dandridge was the one who went with me. That man was totally unafraid of anyone.

I'm not sure how much good it did to have an extra person with me. My face and my 1955 blue Chevy 150 were too easily recognized. We had bought the Chevy soon after we got to Montgomery. Our "miracle Oldsmobile" was about ready to give up.

Once more God showed us that he was in charge of our finances as well as our lives. Our brother-in-law, Bill Deutschmann, had worked as a "stringer" for Ricart Ford while he was in seminary. Bill had informed me about the value of cars so that I would know a bargain when I found one. So I walked confidently into the Chevrolet dealership and told the salesman I wanted his cheapest model with only a heater and radio. "I will pay cash," I said.

"You can have this new one right now for twenty-two hundred dollars," he said.

"I'll take it," I replied. We shook hands on the deal, signed the papers, and I headed to the bank to arrange a loan.

When I told the banker how much I wanted to borrow, he looked at me incredulously. "You must mean you're buying a used car," he said. "You can't buy a new car for twenty-two hundred dollars."

"No," I assured him. "This is a brand new car."

He picked up his phone and called the dealership, then turned back to me in disbelief. "The salesman says you're right. He sold you a new car for twenty-two hundred dollars. But I still don't believe it." Nevertheless, the banker approved the loan.

Within two years our rapidly growing family needed a station wagon, and again the Lord supplied. But the Chevy was the car everyone in

Montgomery seemed to know. Sometimes I wished we had never bought it. One day, while I was driving up Cleveland Avenue, two cars traveling much faster than I pulled up behind me. One of them raced around me just before we all stopped for a traffic signal, sandwiching me between them. The driver, a white man, opened his door, leaned out, and shouted to the man behind me, "That's that nigger-lovin' preacher in front of you!" It was frightening to realize how easily I was recognized.

On another occasion, my good friend Bob Hughes borrowed our car to take a trip out of town because his own was not functioning. On the way home he stopped to eat in Wetumpka. While sitting at the lunch counter, he heard some commotion outside and saw the Ku Klux Klan parading by. Bob was neither disturbed nor surprised. After all, this was Klan country.

Suddenly his complacency vanished. He remembered that he had parked my car right in front of the restaurant. The number 3 in the corner of my license plate indicated that the car came from Montgomery County. To make matters worse, Bob was about my height and build. Fearing that someone from the Klan would recognize my car, come looking for me, and find him inside, he didn't dare go near the car until the parade had passed well out of sight. Then he wasted no time getting out of town.

We had met Bob and Dottie Hughes when we first became involved with the Montgomery Council on Human Relations (MCHR) and its statewide counterpart, the Alabama Council. Bob was the state director, but both he and Dottie took an active part in the local group as well. Those human relations councils indirectly received much of their support from the Ford Foundation.

That connection prompted some absurd reactions. In one case a British news reporter had come to Montgomery to cover the boycott. In order to get a better picture of the total social setting, he had rented a car and traveled around the state, interviewing people as he went. He returned to Montgomery utterly confused.

"I couldn't purchase any petrol!" he told me. "Many places I stopped, they refused to sell me any petrol because I was driving a Ford motor-car."

After I explained the Ford connection, he understood, but he was still flabbergasted. His being a foreigner snooping around probably made the situation worse. I only wish I could have read the story he wrote after he returned home.

In spite of the problems they caused for my British friend, the human relations councils were very important to us. They were among a mere handful of organizations that brought Negro and white people together on a level of equality. When I attended one of the early meetings of the Montgomery Council in the fellowship hall of the Dexter Avenue Baptist Church in downtown Montgomery, I met the pastor of that congregation, who had arrived in town only a few months before we did. He seemed friendly, intelligent, and articulate, and I looked forward to getting better acquainted with him. His name intrigued me— Martin Luther King, Jr.!

In the 1990s it is hard to imagine that simply going to a meeting could be an act of courage. But in the mid-1950s a white person taking part in an integrated organization, especially in the South, defied all social mores and jeopardized the principles that controlled every aspect of life. Tensions were already high because the Southern way of life was under strong attack. Only one year before, the U.S. Supreme Court had declared segregation in public schools unconstitutional. White people feared and resisted any attempt to further erode the institution of segregation.

Businessmen especially had difficulty taking part in groups such as the Montgomery Council. A few of them supported us, but they rarely came to public meetings. More commonly, wives became actively involved in *our* councils, while their husbands took part in White Citizens Councils and other organizations working to preserve segregation. One husband published a legal notice in the newspaper announcing that he did not agree with his wife's positions and had nothing to do with the organizations she supported.

It was not at all unusual to arrive at a meeting of the MCHR and find Montgomery police officers writing down the license numbers of all who went into the meeting. The Negroes had grown accustomed to that kind of intimidation; they had experienced it all of their lives. But it frightened the white people involved, especially those in sensitive positions.

The courage of Bob and Dottie Hughes bolstered the morale of other white people in the councils. Bob, very visible on the front line, never wavered. When their ministry in Alabama ended a few years later, the Hughes family went to another hot spot, a colony in Africa then called Southern Rhodesia. Bob obviously continued his attacks on racism. He was soon ordered by the government to leave the country. He was *persona non grata.*

Another organization I joined soon after our arrival was the Montgomery Ministerial Association. It admitted only white members, of course, but I felt it was important for me to be there. Many of my fellow clergy were working hard to bring about better race relations in their congregations, usually without much success. Most of my close friends among the Methodist ministers were forced to move frequently because Methodists are subject to annual appointment. As soon as their congregations realized they were *"liberals,"* a truly pejorative term then, the ministers were asked to move on.

One of my best friends and supporters in the ministerial association was Pastor Russell Boggs, who served Our Redeemer Lutheran Church.

Some of Russell's members were unhappy with his liberal stance and even more unhappy about his relationship with me. Before we arrived, Russell had come close to causing a riot in his neighborhood. The Boggs family had invited Pastor Nelson Trout and his family to dinner in their home. The new parsonage at Trinity was then just in the planning stage. After dinner, Russell took Nelson to see a newly constructed house for sale on his block. Although he was only trying to give Nelson some ideas for Trinity's new parsonage, his neighbors assumed he was trying to get a Negro family to buy that house.

Russell even invited me to preach at his church on special occasions. I sometimes wondered if he was daring his congregation to try to get rid of him. He demonstrated his courage further when he later left Montgomery, not to serve another congregation, but to become a military chaplain—in the paratroopers!

Some of the white pastors developed "cell groups" of liberal members in their congregations. While I was sitting in the office of a young Presbyterian minister one day, two teenage white boys came in to see him and eyed me suspiciously. I assumed they recognized me and wondered what I was doing in their pastor's office.

The minister noticed their apprehension.

"It's all right," he assured them. "He's one of us."

The boys broke into smiles and began to talk freely.

Participation in the ministerial association had its lighter moments as well. The chaplain at Kilby Prison invited us to come there for one of our monthly meetings. He arranged for us to have lunch in the cafeteria, eating the same food as prisoners, using the same utensils. As we walked past the counters and put food onto our battered metal trays. I served myself a helping of mashed potatoes and some strange-looking gravy. It tasted even stranger than it looked. I sat there thinking about what those poor prisoners had to go through until I noticed the other pastors were eating dessert, and I had none. Their butterscotch pudding may have been good dessert, but it certainly didn't make good gravy!

Membership in the white ministerial association also provided me the opportunity to do devotional programs on local radio and television. I hoped that these programs gave at least some of the listeners a different impression of me than what they saw in the newspapers. While doing the devotional programs, I met some wonderful media people who supported the movement though they were unable to speak out publicly.

One who stands out in my mind was Frank McGee. Then a reporter for the local NBC television station, Frank later became a national news anchor for NBC. But one day Frank confided to me, "It's a good thing I wasn't born a Negro. I see how those people are treated. With my temper, I couldn't take it. I'd get myself killed."

Another Lutheran pastor, who arrived in Montgomery later on, never joined the ministerial association—not because he belonged to the Missouri Synod but because he was not welcome. Bill Griffen was a Negro. My being Lutheran may have caused problems for Russ Boggs but not for Bill. Every time he called on new families, when he announced that he was a Lutheran, the doors opened wide. Everyone knew about that

*Margee and Bobby, with children of Pastor Bill Griffen.*

white Lutheran preacher across town who participated in the boycott.

One day Bill and his wife, Ella Mae, led us on a tour of Missouri Synod congregations in Lowndes County, the heart of the Black Belt (and home of the Dandridge family). Though Negroes far outnumbered whites in that area, the white minority ran everything. At one point on our drive we pulled to the side of the road, and a white man nearby said something.

Bill, sitting in the front with me, turned to me and said, "He wants to talk to you."

"Ask him what he wants," I said.

Bill asked and turned back to me again. "He wants to talk to you, he says."

The conversation continued that way until the white man finally gave up.

We all knew the risks of what we were doing. We were used to that. Surrounded by danger constantly, we had to trust in God's care to make it from day to day. We had no intention of giving in to racism in any form.

Another ministerial group I belonged to, the all-Negro Interdenominational Ministerial Alliance, welcomed Bill Griffen. (White groups were usually called *associations;* Negro groups were called *alliances*.) Baptists and Methodists dominated the Alliance, typical of Negro communities everywhere. No more than a handful of us represented all the other denominations. Though I was not Negro, I was readily admitted to the Alliance since I was pastor of a Negro congregation. I doubt if any of my white predecessors had joined the group.

As a member of both ministerial groups, I tried to bridge the two organizations and the communities they represented.

At one point a few of us in the white organization proposed a joint worship service. After endless debate within the white group, one of our members commented, "I just have one more thing to add before I leave. They say that silence is golden. But sometimes it is just plain yellow."

The conservative ministers still didn't want to take part in the joint worship, but they couldn't let others think they were cowards. The vote to proceed was nearly unanimous.

Interestingly, on the day of the joint service, more conservative white ministers attended than liberals. The liberals already had good contacts with their Negro counterparts, and they had no need to prove they were not cowards.

I had indeed served as a bridge between the liberal white pastors and the Negro leadership. We had developed an informal, ecumenical, interracial, and *illegal* fellowship that covered the entire state. We often discussed the role of the church and the minister in Alabama race relations. On April 6, 1956 I gave that organization an "Analysis of the Present Situation in Montgomery."

Because of the high risk to white participants, we often met in places few white people would go, often campuses of Negro colleges, some of them state-supported. Our presence created problems for the college administrators. The very existence of those institutions depended on their staying in the good graces of white officials and lawmakers. It was essential that nothing on their records indicate that a group such as ours had used their facilities. So each time we met on the campus of a state-supported college, we were their guests—no charge for food, housing, or meeting rooms. Officially we were not there.

In all fairness to the Montgomery Ministerial Association, I should note that in September 1956, after the first bombing of our house, they *did* speak out. Trinity's church log says, "Sept. 10—Montgomery Ministerial Association meeting. Adopted statement for publication which states opposition to 'undisciplined' words and acts which slander racial or religious groups in our population."

Meanwhile, the ministry at Trinity Lutheran Church continued—before, during, and after the bus boycott. In spite of the extraordinary amounts of time other church members and I invested in the movement, the congregation continued to grow. During the three years we served in Montgomery, baptized membership increased by about one-third and confirmed membership increased by about fifteen percent.

One of my greatest joys as a pastor was working with the young people. In the Lutheran Church, usually a two-year period of instruction given at ages twelve to fourteen prepares youngsters for confirmation and full adult membership. So I enjoyed plenty of time with my younger members.

A year after we arrived, we held another Bible camp for the teenagers, again with a visiting speaker. After the boycott had begun I met a young white Lutheran who was visiting Montgomery to see for himself what was happening. At the time, he was editor of a small-town newspaper in southwestern Illinois while serving in the Illinois House of Representatives. He was our visiting speaker. After his presentation to our young people about Christians being involved in politics, I said to the group, "Remember the name Paul Simon. Someday you'll be saying 'President Paul Simon.'"

Over the years I have watched with anticipation as Paul has moved forward one step at a time in his political career, still living out the role of a committed Christian serving his Lord in the arena of politics. As a U.S. Senator, Paul Simon was gearing up for his 1988 presidential campaign, I reminded him of what I had told those Alabama teens in the summer of 1956. The real question, of course, was whether *they* remembered.

More than thirty years later, when Jeannie and I went back to Trinity Lutheran Church, many of those same young people were still active in the congregation, now serving as leaders and teachers. I cannot help but think that every minute we invested in them has yielded greater dividends than we could have imagined.

# 4

## THE DECISION THAT CHANGED OUR LIVES

Our ministry in Montgomery might have remained normal and uneventful if it had not been for a series of events that began on Thursday, December 1, 1955. The following Saturday one of our members called to tell us that a Negro woman had been arrested on a Montgomery bus two days earlier and that people were being asked to boycott the buses for one day, Monday, December 5, in protest.

We had been in Montgomery for less than six months, but we had already observed many of the degrading and demeaning features of racial segregation. Some of the worst stories related to the local bus system, owned and operated by a *northern* company.

Unlike some large Southern cities, Montgomery maintained a rigid pattern of bus segregation. The front ten seats were reserved for white passengers and the last ten for Negroes, seventy percent of the bus-riding public. When the reserved seats were filled, passengers could take adjacent seats. There were never enough white people on board to fill the bus, but no Negro was ever allowed to sit in those front seats, even if there wasn't a single white passenger on board. Usually, Negroes were not even allowed to stand beside the seats reserved for whites.

Especially at the end of the day, when laborers might be dirty and sweaty, bus drivers routinely made Negroes pay their fares at the front and then board through the back door to prevent them from walking past white passengers. They had to move fast, or the bus would drive away before they could reach the back door, particularly if they were pregnant women or older people. Some of the drivers thought it was a big joke when they succeeded in leaving someone behind.

Some drivers, however, were courteous and pleasant, even to the point of waiting at the corner for Negro passengers hurrying to catch the bus.

When the entire bus was filled and more whites boarded, the front row of Negroes had to stand, yielding their seats to the additional white people. The driver would call back, "All right, you niggers, get up!" The blacks almost always complied. Negro women often had to give up their seats for white men. People could not afford the expense of going to jail, and they feared losing their jobs if they caused trouble. The bus was the only means of transportation most of them could afford.

From time to time, some brave soul would refuse to move and would be arrested, jailed, and fined, usually for "disorderly conduct." Three women had already been arrested in 1955 for refusing to give up their seats on Montgomery buses. Several groups had tried to organize a bus boycott in protest, but those plans never succeeded.

The seating arrangements were not the worst feature of riding the city buses, however. Abusive treatment, even violence, caused greater concern. A few drivers delighted in calling Negro passengers "niggers," "black apes," and other insulting names. One day a particularly abusive driver called out, "If it wasn't for these whites sitting up here, I'd wreck this bus and kill every one of you God damn black sons of bitches!"

Sometimes drivers would refuse to make change for Negroes, or they would drop the change or transfers on the floor instead of into the black passengers' hands. Negroes presenting transfers would occasionally be told they had to pay again.

The physical abuse was also devastating. A woman with two infants boarded a bus one day and stood at the front while she took the fare money out of her purse. When the driver saw that the children had climbed onto one of the front seats, he started driving, then slammed on his brakes, throwing the little babies to the floor.

On another occasion, a Negro man boarded a bus on the square in downtown Montgomery. After an altercation, the driver called the police, a fairly common occurrence. But this time was different. As the man was brought off the bus, one of the policemen shot him. The coroner's report called it *justifiable homicide*.

Virtually every Negro in Montgomery either had experienced bad treatment on the buses or knew people who had.

After receiving news of the proposed boycott, I wanted to learn more, so I called a friend who lived around the corner from us in the Cleveland Court Apartments. Mrs. Rosa Parks was the adult advisor to the Montgomery NAACP Youth Council, which met in our church building. I dialed her number.

After exchanging greetings, I said, "I just heard that someone was arrested on one of the buses Thursday."

"That's right, Pastor Graetz."

"And that we're supposed to boycott the buses on Monday to protest."

"That's right, Pastor Graetz."

"Do you know anything about it?"

"Yes, Pastor Graetz."

"Do you know who was arrested?"

"Yes, Pastor Graetz."

"Well, who was it?"

There was a moment of silence. Then in a quiet, timid voice she replied, "It was me, Pastor Graetz."

It would have been unlike her to respond in any other way. Mrs. Rosa Parks was dignified and reserved, one of the most highly respected people in the Negro community. For years she had quietly grieved over the harsh treatment her people had received at the hands of whites, and she worked hard as secretary of the Alabama chapter of the NAACP to bring about changes in the segregation system. Earlier that year at Highlander Folk School in Monteagle, Tennessee, she had been inspired to take some kind of positive action.

On the phone she explained what happened. Having had a difficult day as a seamstress in a downtown department store, she was tired, and she held several packages in her lap. Sick of the treatment her people had been receiving on the buses, she could not allow herself to give up her seat even one more time. Her action was not premeditated. It just happened.

Not long after my conversation with Mrs. Parks, someone brought us one of the boycott flyers which had been distributed in the Negro community. It read:

Don't ride the bus to work, to town, to school, or any place Monday, December 5.

Another Negro woman has been arrested and put in jail because she refused to give up her bus seat.

Don't ride the buses to work, to town, to school, or anywhere on Monday. If you work, take a cab, or share a ride, or walk.

Come to a mass meeting, Monday at 7:00 P.M., at the Holt Street Baptist Church for further instruction.

Thousands of copies of an earlier, longer message had been distributed all over town by the Women's Political Council, primarily well-to-do professional women committed to fighting segregation in any form. One of their members, elderly Mrs. A. W. West, wife of a Montgomery dentist, made quite a spectacle during the early days of the boycott, driving people to and from work each day in her Cadillac!

With the boycott imminent Jeannie and I had a decision to make. I had promised our church officials that I would concentrate on being a pastor and would not start trouble. I did not want to violate the spirit of my agreement, so in response to this call for action, we sought God's guidance. During the rest of that day, we prayed off and on, asking God what our role should be and what I should say to our congregation on Sunday morning.

Soon the answer was clear. We had to be involved. Afterward, we realized that if we had remained aloof, our effectiveness in the Negro community would have disintegrated. We would have had to pack up and move out. Though we realized that our decision put our entire family in danger, we intended to do whatever our Lord told us.

Sunday morning the people who gathered at Trinity Lutheran Church shared the emotions experienced in churches all over town. I'm sure my announcement echoed dozens of others.

"As you no doubt know, Mrs. Rosa Parks was arrested on Thursday for refusing to give up her seat on a city bus to a white man. The Negro leaders of Montgomery have called for a boycott of the buses tomorrow to protest her arrest and the bad treatment of many people on the buses. I am appealing to every one of you to take part in this boycott. Share the ride tomorrow. I will be out with my car early in the morning, driving people to work. Jeannie will be by the phone at home. If you need a ride, please call.

"Let's try to make this boycott as effective as possible because it won't be any boycott if half of us ride the buses and half don't ride. So if we're going to do it, let's make a good job of it."

There was no turning back for us. We had not only taken residence among the Negro people of Montgomery, but from that point on, their struggle became our own.

That weekend a minor event played a key role in the success of the boycott. A Negro maid who had received one of the flyers asked her employer if she might have Monday off. When asked why, the maid brought out the flyer and showed it to her.

The white woman was shocked but pleased at the opportunity to undercut the plans of the "colored" people. "You can have Monday off if you let me have that paper," she said.

The employer hurried to the office of the *Montgomery Advertiser* and headed for the desk of Joe Azbell, the City Editor. "Look at this," she cried.

Instantly Joe had a front-page story for Sunday's paper. The headline read: "Negroes to Boycott Buses Monday." Joe Azbell's straightforward article reported the arrest of Mrs. Parks, the proposed one-day boycott, and the meeting planned for Monday evening. He would cover the meeting himself.

As the news spread over the weekend, many of Montgomery's Negroes doubted whether the boycott would work. Such plans had been talked about for years with no results. Dr. King and the other leaders experienced misgivings about how their people would respond.

But excitement grew as Negroes in home after home picked up their papers from their porches on Sunday morning and read the front-page story. "I guess it really *is* going to happen," they said.

As I left the house Monday morning, *my* excitement mingled with awe and fear. I knew I was helping with something important, not only to our own church members but to the entire Negro community. Yet no one knew how the white community would react.

I began cruising the streets, picking up people on their way to work. Incredibly, within minutes I could see that these were not the same people I had come to know in the few months we had lived in Montgomery. Overnight they had transformed.

Through the years we have observed four mind-sets in Negro communities, which, though oversimplified here, help explain the enormous change that took place.

The first mind-set was "pre-December 5, 1955, Montgomery." Though certainly not everyone fit the pattern, we saw many Negro people who had essentially given up. They seemed to be saying, "We're 'colored.' We're not much good to ourselves or anybody else. It's awful the way we have to live, but it's never going to change. We might as well try to get along as well as we can and do what the white folks say. Someday God's going to take us across the Jordan River, and everything will be better."

We couldn't blame people for feeling that way. Whites wielded virtually all political and economic power. Negroes had little or no influence in critical decisions regarding their own lives. The image of Stephen Foster's "Old Black Joe" still thrived in the South. Although large numbers of Negroes never allowed themselves to fall into this thought pattern, many others did.

There were always Negroes even during the period of legal slavery, whose spirits were never broken, resisting their inhumane treatment at every opportunity. This included those already released, but who still sacrificed their own lives and freedom for the sake of their race. In 1955, Montgomery also had its share of courageous people.

We saw the second mind-set in California: Negroes in our congregation and community trying to escape from their own identity. *Race* was a four-letter word rarely spoken in public. Activities that brought together Negro and white people were *intercultural,* never *interracial.* No one dared to call Community Lutheran a Negro church.

When a missionary spoke to us one Sunday, I watched our members freeze into shocked silence when she said, "I'm delighted to see all your brown faces. It takes me back to Africa."

Our people didn't want anyone to know they had any connection with Africa. They seemed to be saying, "We used to think of ourselves as Negroes. But now we have escaped from our past. We want to merge into the majority community and forget about where we came from. We will give up everything just to be accepted."

We found the third mind-set in Columbus, Ohio. In housing patterns, Columbus was the second-most-segregated city in the nation, second only to Chicago. Even after the legal barriers had been broken down, banks and realtors cooperated to preserve the "integrity" and "property values" of white neighborhoods.

As late as the 1960s, members of St. Philips Church had difficulty finding decent homes. One family with a comfortable income tried to buy land outside of town. To their horror, they discovered that the restriction applied even in the country. No land was available *to them*.

Though the employment scene had improved, still many jobs were either closed to Negroes or severely limited.

But the Negro people of Columbus did not deny their heritage. They said in effect, "Because we are Negroes, we have additional problems to face. But we will not be defeated. We will not deny who we are. We'll make the most of every opportunity and keep moving ahead."

These comparisons are unfair, of course. The social settings and legal patterns differed greatly. And people's personal experiences molded their attitudes. But perhaps these descriptions can help white people better understand what their Negro brothers and sisters were going through.

And mind-sets can change. The fourth mind-set appeared in Montgomery on December 5, 1955. As I cruised the streets that Monday morning, I saw Negro people striding along as if they didn't have a care in the world, their heads held high, their faces covered with smiles. They seemed unconcerned about whether they walked or rode. What they were doing was more important than how or when they reached their destination. I had never seen such proud, confident, happy people.

Their message was clear: "We are colored, Negro, black. We are whatever we decide we are. We are people of value and worth. With God's help we will determine our own destiny, no longer allowing white people to push us around as if they owned us. Whatever they may do to us, we will not be afraid."

A new day had dawned in Montgomery. We didn't know it at the time, but a new day had dawned for America as well. Though for many decades before December 5, 1955, many individual Negroes had fit this pattern, never before had this spirit been so pervasive.

Another factor contributed to the boycott's success. Rumors spread through the white community that Negro "goon squads" would roam the streets, forcibly keeping people off the buses. To prevent this the police department assigned two motorcycle officers to follow each bus that drove into a Negro neighborhood. According to the *Advertiser* that morning, city officials promised to "call out every city policeman and every reserve policeman, if necessary, to maintain law and order."

A handful of Negro people had decided to ride the buses in spite of the boycott, but most changed their minds when they saw the motorcycles. One potential rider said, "Look at that! They even have the police out to make sure we don't get on the buses."

The boycott was nearly one hundred percent effective, exceeding the wildest dreams of those who had proposed it.

Dr. King said later that he would have considered a sixty-percent response a success. But when he and his wife, Coretta, watched the first bus roll by their South Jackson Street home at 6:00 A.M, it was empty!

Mr. Robert Dandridge called us later in the day. "I've been sitting on my porch since early this morning, watching the buses drive by," he said, "And they're as naked as they can be!"

One old man said, "Pastor Graetz, this is the first time our people have stuck together in anything."

That afternoon the *Alabama Journal* reported:

> At 5:30 A.M. today the big yellow busses of the Montgomery City Lines began pulling into Court Square to pick up passengers.
> Generally a swarm of Negro passengers are waiting at the stop for

the busses to take them to the railroad shops, private homes, laundries, factories, and jobs throughout the city. . . .

Negroes were on almost every corner in the downtown area silent, waiting for rides or moving about to keep warm, but few got on buses.

One of the local papers carried a picture of a crudely lettered sign: "Remember We Are Fighting for a Cause. Do Not Ride a Bus Today."

Mid-morning I stopped hauling passengers and headed for the courtroom downtown where Mrs. Parks was to go on trial for violating the bus segregation law. Because she had remained perfectly calm during her violation and arrest, offering no resistance, the arresting officers had not charged her with disorderly conduct, the usual charge. The difference in her citation encouraged us to challenge the segregation law itself.

Arriving at the courtroom, I violated my own rule about never making use of a segregated facility. In those days, even the courts provided separate seating for whites and Negroes. The only way I could observe the trial was to sit in the white section. Feeling very uncomfortable, I went in. The entire space reserved for Negroes was filled, and many more people stood outside. But I had no trouble finding a seat in the white section. As Mrs. Parks's trial was about to begin, the conversations I overheard made me even more nervous. I was surrounded by hostile whites.

"Which one is the nigger lawyer?" someone asked.

"It's the yellow one up in front there," came the response.

That was my introduction to attorney Fred Gray, who was representing Mrs. Parks. Over time he became one of our closest friends and coworkers.

Seven months later I served as an usher when Fred married Bernice Hill. Since the South's segregation laws covered almost all public activities, my very participation was against the law. Besides being illegal, my involvement in their wedding created some complications for Fred and Bernice. Their plans for a formal wedding dictated tuxedos for the men. A white man owned the one store in Montgomery which rented tuxedos. He was perfectly happy to do business with Negroes, even with the notorious Attorney Gray, but he might have balked at complicity in my illegal involvement. So Fred got my measurements and told the store owner that his other usher would not be able to come in for a fitting. We took our chances that the tux would fit.

At Mrs. Parks's trial, Fred said little, since the outcome of the trial was never in doubt and Fred could do nothing to change it. But as the boycott moved along, he kept quite busy providing legal assistance to our organization. Judge John Scott wasted no time finding Mrs. Parks guilty, fining her ten dollars plus court costs, a total of fourteen dollars. After Fred announced his intention to appeal the conviction, the trial ended.

I don't remember how much more driving I did that day. I wanted to hurry home to share with Jeannie the experiences of the morning. And I wanted to get to the meeting at Holt Street Baptist Church plenty early. Mr. Dandridge and I planned to go together. (I could always count on him.)

But what a surprise when we arrived at the church! The doorway, the sidewalk, and even the street were filled with people, all Negroes except for some city police officers, as far as I could tell.

Joe Azbell reported in the next day's *Advertiser* that five thousand Negroes attended. He added, "There were four white reporters or photographers at the meeting. Only one other white person attended. He appeared to be a young college student or airman [there were two air force bases outside of Montgomery] and he came with a Negro and left with a Negro. He sat in the group of Negroes in the balcony."

I assumed Joe Azbell had seen me, but not long after that, I met a white airman from Maxwell Air Force Base who attended every mass meeting, taking notes on all the proceedings.

Seeing the huge crowd, I was glad there were loudspeakers outside the building. At least we could hear what was going on inside. But Mr. Dandridge was not about to let his pastor stand on the outside of such an important function as this. He led me through the crowd. Since he was recognized as one of the patriarchs of black Montgomery, everyone let us go through.

Reaching the inside of the building, we saw no way to get into the worship center, so we listened from the fellowship hall as people sang and prayed upstairs.

After accomplishing the seemingly impossible, carrying out a nearly perfect boycott of the city's buses with no violence and no major difficulties, the Negro people of Montgomery were in a truly festive mood. Because of the crowds thronging every portion of the church building, it took a long time for Dr. King and the other leaders to reach the front of the sanctuary. But no one minded. That crowd wouldn't have cared if the meeting had lasted all night.

The proceedings finally began with a hymn and a prayer. Soon I recognized a voice on the loudspeaker, that of the minister from the Dexter Avenue Baptist Church, Dr. Martin Luther King, Jr. His words galvanized the crowd.

He talked about what had happened to Mrs. Parks and about the general treatment of Negroes on the buses and elsewhere. As Dr. King discussed the day's activities, he used a word that had not come up before, *protest*.

During the months that we stayed off the buses, we avoided the negative connotations of the term *boycott*, calling our actions a *protest movement*. We were not attempting to penalize the bus company for their past sins, merely protesting injustice.

Dr. King told the crowd that they should not stoop to treating white people the way white people had treated them. He closed by saying, "If you will protest courageously, and yet with dignity and Christian love, when the history books are written in future generations, the historians will have to pause and say, 'There lived a great people—a black people—who injected new meaning and dignity into the veins of civilization.' This is our challenge and our overwhelming responsibility."

I heard those words echoed in many mass meetings after that. Speakers would say, "Let the history books record that there was a people in Montgomery, Alabama—a black people . . ." and the crowd would roar its approval.

After Dr. King's address, Mrs. Parks, sitting in the front row, was introduced. This gentle woman's quiet dignity and courage had inspired fifty thousand Negroes to stand up for their human rights, to stand together, imbued with their own dignity and courage. And that night they stood together to give her an ovation.

Then Rev. Ralph Abernathy presented the only items of business that night. The first question put to the assembly: "Do you want to end the protest and get back on the buses?"

"No, no!" came the resounding chorus.

Ralph then read a resolution including three demands the bus company would have to meet before Montgomery's Negroes would return to the buses:

(1) A guarantee of courteous treatment to be given to all passengers.

(2) Passengers to be seated on a first-come, first-served basis, with Negroes starting from the back and whites from the front. Wherever the two groups met, the line would be drawn. Negroes would no longer have to give up their seats if additional white passengers got on the bus.

(3) Negro drivers to be hired for the routes which went primarily into Negro communities.

The resolution was adopted unanimously.

The mild nature of the demands drew no argument that night. Though Dr. King had talked about the evils of segregation, the resolution asked for only a *change* in the segregated system, not its demise. For that reason the National Association for the Advancement of Colored People at first refused to support the Montgomery protest. Some national NAACP leaders were appalled at our meekness. Ultimately, we realized that our "meekness" was providential.

White leaders responded to our demands by saying they could do nothing about the seating system mandated by law. "If you don't like the law, change it," they said. They knew we couldn't, however, because no Negroes participated in the legislative process at that time. But weeks later, when nothing was done about our mild demands, a suit was filed by Fred Gray in federal court, challenging the constitutionality of Alabama's bus segregation law.

One more announcement was made before the mass meeting ended. A new organization called the Montgomery Improvement Association had been formed that afternoon to provide leadership for the protest. Dr. Martin Luther King, Jr., had been elected president.

The MIA board faced some incredibly difficult tasks at the start. Not only did they have to negotiate with city and bus company officials, now that the protest would continue, they also had to develop procedures for getting people to work and to shopping. This movement might last for weeks. It was December. We were heading into the worst of our winter weather.

None of us dreamed that more than a year would pass before the buses would integrate and our protest would end.

The MIA board made transportation and finances top priorities. Negro taxis in Montgomery had given people rides on the first day for ten cents, the same as bus fare, but they could not continue that practice. Our volunteer car pool had also worked well on the first day, but making that work for any length of time required good coordination. The board set up committees to raise money and to establish a regular schedule for the volunteer car pool. Committee members worked almost around the clock for the first week or so.

Our phone rang about 2:00 one morning, and the transportation committee gave me my assignment. They told me the route I was to drive and the hours I should be there. For the next several weeks I drove people to work from 6:00 to 9:00 every morning. Though I had already volunteered, the committee seemed timid about asking me to do much. Others put in many more hours than I did.

Few of the five thousand people at that meeting in the Holt Street Baptist Church thought about practical problems. The vast majority were too intent on celebrating the miracle. Fifty thousand black people had stood against their oppressors, not counting the cost. Proud of what they had begun, they would let nothing turn them back. One of the songs of the movement expressed Montgomery's heartfelt cry: "Ain't gonna let nobody turn me 'round, turn me 'round; I'm headin' for the Freedom Land!"

The meeting now ended, Mr. Dandridge and I slowly moved with the crowd out of the building. Many people greeted Mr. Dandridge. Few knew who I was, so he introduced me to his friends as we inched along.

One man shook my hand and smiled broadly. "Did you enjoy the meeting?" he asked.

"Enjoy it?" snapped Mr. Dandridge. "He's part of it!"

Mr. Dandridge was right. Years before, I had dreamed of pretending I was a Negro to become more involved in the fight for justice. Now I was part of a Negro movement destined to launch the modern civil rights movement in America.

# 5

## EXPOSED

Though it was extremely unlikely, I *could* have continued to be involved in the Montgomery bus protest without the white community knowing.

Negroes in Montgomery, as elsewhere, rarely shared information with white people which should be kept within their own ranks. The Negro community's grapevine would quickly transmit news from house to house but no farther. We witnessed its effectiveness when our house was bombed for the first time.

On August 25, 1956, Jeannie and I, along with our children and Mrs. Rosa Parks, were attending a workshop at the Highlander Folk School in Monteagle, Tennessee. From the time of that school's 1932 founding, director Myles Horton, his wife, and his coworkers had sought to develop bridges of understanding and communication between laboring people and their employers. In the 1950s they focused on race relations.

Early on Saturday morning, the last day of the workshop, a knock on our cabin door woke us. One of Highlander's staffers told us we had a long distance phone call. When I reached the phone, Ted Poston, a Negro reporter for the *New York Post,* broke the news: our house had been bombed.

The story had come over the news wires, and he had called the Montgomery Police Department and other white officials, but no one knew where we were. Then he phoned a Negro friend in Montgomery.

"Why, every Negro in town knows where they are," his friend said.

Within minutes Ted Poston had us on the phone.

A few, of course, violated the code of ethics that protected Negro secrets. Since the days of slavery every community had had its informers. Though such persons were scarce during the bus protest, a few would carry information to "the man" in exchange for personal favors.

Sometimes Negroes could turn the work of informers to their own advantage. Mr. Dandridge told us about something that had happened when he was a young man in Lowndes County.

In spite of a white minority's total control there, a number of "colored" families owned their own plantations. When institutionalized slavery ended, some of the more conscientious slave owners allowed former slaves to buy plantation land for their own use.

The Dandridge family, having worked their own land for many years, was economically independent. Proud and bold, they wouldn't let white people push them around. The Dandridges kept to themselves and let it be known that they would not take kindly to outside interference from any source.

On one occasion a member of the Dandridge family somehow aroused the anger of a few white people in town. In those days "uppity niggers" were punished swiftly to remind all "colored" people that whites were still in charge. The townsmen got together and planned to go out to the Dandridge plantation that night to give the offender a whipping and teach him a lesson. The efficient grapevine alerted the Dandridge family almost as soon as the plans had been made.

Mr. Dandridge's family did two things. First, they called their neighbors and friends together and persuaded them to gather in the fields around their home with pitchforks, shotguns—whatever weapons they had—to protect the potential victim. Second, they made certain there were some local informers present during the conversations.

Then they laughed heartily as they watched their unwitting informers hurry off into town, knowing the message they would convey: "You—all better not go out there to that place. Them crazy niggers are hiding all over the place with guns and everything else."

The Dandridges never heard another word about the alleged offense.

As far as I know, no informer ever betrayed me even though virtually every Negro in Montgomery knew about my participation in the movement.

I didn't try to keep it a secret—quite the contrary. On December 7, just two days after the bus protest began, I sent a mimeographed letter to every member of the (white) Montgomery Ministerial Association.

> Dear Christian Brother:
>
> I am certain that you are aware of the great tension that hangs like a cloud over our city, which has manifested itself particularly in the so-called 'boycott' of the city buses by the Negro people of Montgomery. And I am certain that you are interested in keeping peace between the races and in seeing that all parties concerned are treated justly.

I explained that "the Negroes of Montgomery are not protesting segregation of the buses as such" but were protesting the unfair and unjust treatment they regularly received. Enclosing a copy of the resolution adopted the previous Monday evening, I asked them to study it and communicate their reactions to the bus company. Further, I requested that they keep their congregations "correctly informed." My closing appeal:

> Please consider this matter prayerfully and carefully, with Christian love. Our Lord said, "Inasmuch as ye have done it unto one of the least of these my brethren, ye have done it unto me."

A week later I sent another letter to my brother pastors, clarifying the state law regarding bus segregation and trying to set the record straight after city and bus company officials released some misleading statements to the press. Again I appealed to them to communicate their concerns to our city officials and to the bus company, naively believing that a few of the pastors would have the courage to speak up.

Later I realized that was too much to expect. If our supporters had spoken up, they would not have been with us long. Their congregations would have quickly sent them packing.

Under any circumstances, I could not have remained hidden for long, especially since I was driving in the car pool each day for several hours. The *Alabama Journal* reported on December 5: "At least one white man was carrying Negroes in his automobile and parked in the downtown area until he got a load."

As a matter of fact, one person in particular became outraged when he saw what I was doing. In the *Montgomery Advertiser* on Tuesday, January 10, 1956, reporter Tom Johnson described what happened:

> Graetz hauled as many as 40 or 50 passengers a day, while driving some 50 miles. When he was offered money, he carefully decline[d] to accept it, suggesting that the passenger "multiply the number of rides by 10 cents" [the current bus fare] and contribute that amount at the mass meetings. It was during this period that Graetz had his brush with the law.
>
> As he tells the story, Graetz had been driving about two and one-half hours on the morning of Dec. 19 when he parked by a meter near Dean's Drug Store on Monroe Street [one of the few Negro businesses in downtown Montgomery] to pick up five Negroes going to Normandale, a shopping mall in a white section of Montgomery. He was careful not to park in a nearby taxi zone.
>
> As he crossed Dexter Avenue, a siren sounded from the car behind him and he pulled to the curb. A man who Graetz said he later learned was Sheriff Mac Sim Butler walked up and said: "What are you doing—running a taxi?"
>
> Graetz explained the Negroes were "friends" and not passengers. Butler accused him of picking up passengers in a taxi zone and ordered Graetz to follow him to the county jail.
>
> There, Graetz was placed in a room marked "deputy sheriff" and left alone for a few minutes. "For which I was very grateful," Graetz says. "I had a little prayer session."
>
> Another man who Graetz assumed was a deputy came in and lectured him on religion, politics, and patriotism. "We like things the way they are here," he said. "We don't want anybody trying to change them."

Shortly, Graetz said, Butler returned from the courthouse and said he had tried to charge the minister with running a taxi and hauling Negroes in violation of segregation laws but "the judge wouldn't let him."

He was not threatened, says Graetz, but "they were very rough and gruff."

He was released after about a half hour "under the definite impression they didn't like what I was doing," he recalls wryly.

Though Sheriff Butler may have already known about me, he still appeared shocked and surprised as we came face to face. When we entered his office after the arrest, he made a phone call. "Hello, this is Mac Sim Butler. I've got a man in here who was hauling niggers. . . . Yes, but this is a white man!"

Before releasing me, the sheriff lectured me. "I don't see how you can claim to be a Christian and a minister and believe the things you believe," he said bitterly.

I didn't tell the reporter that when I found myself in the room alone with the gorilla-like deputy, I felt certain I was going to get beaten up. Worse things had happened to other people. I felt my turn had come. I was frightened, but I would have to take it.

As soon as the sheriff released me, I raced back to Dean's Drug Store to report what had happened. But the account of my five passengers had already mobilized the Negro community to rescue me from the sheriff. Some people were already on their way to the courthouse to post bond. They realized even better than I did that if I were placed in the white section of the segregated jail, I may not have come out alive.

More than twenty years later I relived that confrontation with Sheriff Butler when our family traveled to Detroit, Michigan, to see a production of the musical play *Selma,* a depiction of the Montgomery movement and later events in King's life, including his assassination. What an incredible experience it was to watch actor David Adams portraying *me* on the stage.

But being interviewed by reporter Tom Johnson for that feature story was a brand new experience for me.

My log contains this entry for January 10: "Tom Johnson's article appeared in *Advertiser* this morning. Three columns on editorial page—well written." The log *didn't* mention the flood of phone calls that started coming into our home, first at 2:15 A.M. the morning the article appeared. On the note pad beside the phone I wrote: "Jan. 10, 2:15 A.M.—White man who seemed to be drunk. Demanded that I come and give him taxi service like what has been furnished to the dark complected people. Suggested that we set up car pool for white people so can save the ten-cent fare. Refused to give name but called himself Roger."

Since the papers would not have reached the streets or homes yet, our first caller was likely an employee of the *Advertiser*. As a matter of fact, when our house and several other buildings were bombed one year later, some of those implicated in the bombings worked for the paper.

Our first threatening call did not come until 3:35 that afternoon. Such calls would soon become part of our daily routine. I reported the call immediately to F.B.I. Agent Woodrow E. Draut, and to Captain E. P. Brown of the Montgomery Police Department.

We would also be the target of many *insulting* calls as well. The first of those reached us that evening. The caller said, "Pastor, if I was you, I wouldn't call myself a pastor. You're a no-good, nigger-lovin' son-of-a-bitch." It was a different voice from the one who had made the threatening call, who himself had called back several times.

On January 12, Tom Johnson wrote a follow-up to his earlier column:

> After the *Advertiser,* containing the story of his ministry at a Negro Lutheran church on Cleveland Avenue, appeared in general circulation a few hours later, Graetz was besieged by the after-clap of a surprised, and in many cases angry, indignant, white citizenry.
>
> And he, in turn, was surprised by the number who called to express their support of his work. A few dropped by to speak to him in person.
>
> As of late yesterday, Pastor Graetz had logged thirty telephone calls as a direct result of his boycott activities becoming known.
>
> Twelve whites and nine Negroes made friendly calls. Eight calls

were of the unfriendly sort, four of them downright hostile.

At 3:35 P.M. Tuesday a caller threatened that "something might happen" unless Graetz got "out of town by nightfall." Two hours later, three other calls came from the same person in quick succession.

By that time Graetz had informed police and a couple of detectives were on hand. When the phone rang the last time, Graetz quickly passed it to one of the officers, who grinned and said: "I heard him all right."

Not all of the calls were negative. One came as a pleasant surprise. Tom Johnson reported it this way:

Some time later, Graetz received one of the "nicest calls" since his troubles began. The caller was Police Commission[er] Clyde Sellers, who had learned of the threats shortly after the young pastor called the police.

Almost immediately, Graetz says, Sellers told him: "you know I don't agree with what you believe but I do believe that every man has the right to his own beliefs."

Then Sellers, a White Citizens Council member, assured Graetz, the former NAACP organizer, that nothing would happen to him, that police cars would watch the pastorate all night to discourage any violence."

Over the next few days, the phone rang almost constantly, subjecting us to a variety of harassing tactics. Some folks would call and then hang up as soon as we answered, especially in the middle of the night. We took care of that problem by putting the phone on the couch at bedtime, covering it with a pillow. If our friends needed to reach us at night, they knew they had to let the phone ring long enough for us to hear its muffled sound.

When anonymous callers gave any indication that they were willing to talk, I tried to engage them in reasonable conversations, which rarely lasted long.

Soon the callers would recover their equilibrium and say, "Yes, but you are a communist, aren't you?" The great red menace overshadowed any other consideration.

The majority of calls actually supported us. Most of our close white friends called, and many others who phoned soon became our friends. One woman identified herself as an "old white lady" from an old Southern family, who was "right with us." She even offered the use of her automobile.

The support of dozens of such people helped us keep perspective in the garbage heap of threats and insults.

Tom Johnson's column, especially after it hit the news wires, elicited more than phone calls. As the days went by, our poor mail carrier probably heaved a great sigh of relief after he delivered our mail each day. Our first anonymous letter was short and to the point:

> May you have for a son-in-law the blackest Negro that ever originated in the wilds of Africa.

The letter had come from Union Springs, Alabama. Its writer wanted to leave no doubt about his identity. He signed it, "A White Man," underlined three times.

In those days, the worst imaginable fate in the minds of segregationists was what they called *mongrelization*, by which they meant the mixing of the races.

Letters were delivered to us addressed simply: Lutheran Minister, Montgomery, Alabama. They poured in from virtually every state in the country, including all parts of Dixie. We also received mail from Europe, Asia, and Africa.

Most heartening was the flood of mail from ministers and church people, including many of my classmates in the seminary. Gifts came for the movement, for our church, and for us.

Jeannie and I were particularly moved by a resolution adopted by the Board of American Missions of our American Lutheran Church:

> The Board commends you for the calm and deliberate way in which
> you applied the Gospel and carried on your ministry in the unpredicted

and unexpected situations that arose.

We are petitioning our gracious Heavenly Father to give you the wisdom and guidance, the courage and insight necessary to continue to be a true shepherd in the full spirit of Jesus Christ.

Two moving letters came from small children in a Quaker Sunday school in Milwaukee, Wisconsin:

Dear. Rev. Graetz,

We are glad you are helping the people of the South to become better friends.

Yours truly,

Nancy Harlan

Dear Rev. Graetz,

We have learned in our Friends Sunday school about the Negroes and their trouble in the South. I am very sorry of the trouble and would like to help in it. I hope you are coming along well with helping the Negroes. Our class sends you our best wishes.

Truly yours

Erich F.

Coincidentally, the three-day Alabama Lutheran Pastoral Conference met at Trinity on January 10, the very day Tom Johnson's column appeared. Our friend Jim Darnell from Birmingham, the only other white minister in the conference, was staying in our home.

About 2:00 A.M. on January 12 we woke to the sound of a crash in front of the house. Jim and Jeannie and I rushed to the picture window in the living room and looked out toward the street. Within seconds we heard the sounds of a car driving away, barely navigable, dragging some of its parts along very loudly.

The car had apparently been speeding down Georgia Street, which came to a dead end in front of our house. Failing to negotiate the turn, the car had jumped the curb and rammed into the bank about halfway up. (Jeannie still believes the occupants had come to do some kind of mischief and missed the opportunity because of their own carelessness.)

Realizing there was no longer any danger, the three of us relaxed and looked at each other and began to snicker. It was rather warm in Alabama that January, and Jim and I had worn boxer shorts for pajamas. Jeannie, who was nine-months pregnant (she would give birth to our daughter Dianne just twelve days later), was wearing a short nightie. After a hearty laugh, we all headed back to bed. We must have made quite a sight for anyone who happened to look in the picture window of our house that night.

At first we rarely closed the drapes over the picture window. But that practice changed rather quickly after we started getting phone calls from people who described what they saw us doing in our living room. When we closed the drapes, they called to dare us to open them. One called said, "Pastor Graetz, you're a no-good son of a bitch if you don't open them blinds. I got something for you." We knew that someone was watching us closely, possibly someone who lived on that first block of Georgia Street.

Though we lived in a Negro neighborhood, there were white families less than a hundred yards away. Racially segregated housing in the South was significantly different from that in the North. Northern segregation tended to isolate Negroes or other unwanted groups in ghettos separated from white neighborhoods by natural barriers. Housing patterns in the South reflected plantation life in the days of slavery. Slaves' shanties were generally located close to the master's "big house." It was not unusual in the 1950s to find on one street a row of nice homes owned by white people, and on the next street, smaller, poorer homes occupied by Negroes. A truism of the times reflected the different thinking: In the South whites said to Negroes, "You can get as close as you want as long as you don't get too high" and in the North they said, "You can get as high as you want as long as you don't get too close."

The homes on Cleveland Avenue, our street, were all occupied by Negro families. But Georgia Street, which began in front of our house and went east, was a white neighborhood. Some of the people in homes we could see from our front window had to be among those making the nasty and threatening phone calls.

The calls were bad enough, but there was more. Before the end of the week we had an unwelcome nighttime visitor. One morning, as I started to get into our car, the possibility of vandalism didn't enter my mind. But when I looked closer, I found that the little pile of white, granular, sticky stuff lay directly under the filling spout of the gas tank. On removing the cap, I found more inside.

*Sugar!* It had to be sugar. I had heard that putting sugar into a gas tank was a sure way to ruin an engine. On inquiry, I was advised not even to drive the car into the shop. Before long, a tow truck was hauling our poor car into the service department of Capitol Chevrolet.

Later that day, I walked the mile or so into town to check on the repairs. The car was on the hoist. Mechanics had removed the gas tank and cleaned it out, and they were in the process of reinstalling it. As I stood off to the side watching, another workman walked past, whispering to follow him. Having no idea what was going on, I walked around the corner with him.

"Don't ever tell anyone I told you this," he warned, "but I just don't like to see anyone get hurt. Whoever put that sugar in your gas tank also slashed your front tires. They cut them on the inside where you wouldn't notice. Now you stay here for a minute. Don't let anyone see me with you." With that he walked away.

I didn't even look at the tires while I was still in the shop. I was afraid someone might realize my anonymous friend had warned me. But when I got home, I crawled under the car and found out he was right. Both front tires had been slashed several times on the inside, not quite deep enough to puncture them. The vandals probably counted on the tires heating up and blowing out when I was out on the highway, when it would be the most dangerous. We didn't know whether the slasher was the same one who put the sugar in the gas tank or perhaps one of the mechanics at the shop. Our enemies were everywhere, as were our secret friends and supporters. We just couldn't always be sure which was which.

A few days later, we received a phone call which seemed to give us an answer. "Is Rev. Graetz in? . . . Do you think that sugar messed up your motor? . . . Do you think that knife cut your tires? . . . Just wait till I get through with you now, Buddy."

He and others certainly were not through with us. But neither was God. Many times we heard older "colored" folks say, "God will make a way where there is no way." Our Lord repeatedly proved that.

After getting the gas tank cleaned and the tires replaced, we visited the auto insurance office to file a claim. Our agent greeted us somberly. "You have to decide for yourself what you want to do," he said. "But I need to warn you that the company will almost surely cancel your policy after they pay this claim."

"What a dilemma," I moaned. "Either we pay for our own damages or we lose our insurance."

Finally we decided we could not afford to pay even the relatively small amount the repairs and tires would cost. We would have to take the risk of losing our insurance coverage. Little did we suspect it didn't matter what we did.

Within days our agent called with the bad news. "Your policy has been canceled," he said, "but I've already transferred you to a different company."

Naively we thought that was the end of the matter. Unfortunately he had to call us again with the same news every few weeks.

Finally one day he said, "I've run out of companies, but I've switched you over to another Negro agent in Birmingham, who has more contacts."

Eventually our Birmingham agent exhausted his list of companies too, but he explained how we could still get coverage. "You'll have to go through the state to get an assigned-risk policy." Each company had to write a certain number of policies on people who could not otherwise get coverage. The number depended on how much business the companies did in Alabama. The rates would likely be high, the agent warned, but at least we would be covered. Ironically, because our record was totally clean, our new premiums turned out to be no higher than before.

While the insurance companies responded negatively to our involvement in the bus protest, churches in general and our own denomination in particular supported us wholeheartedly.

The day after its publication on January 10, Tom Johnson's article went out over the Associated Press wires to newspapers and other media all over the country. I received a letter dated January 16 from Erik Modean, news bureau director for the National Lutheran Council:

> Last Thursday's *New York Times* carried a picture that I've waited for many, many years to see in a newspaper—that of a Lutheran pastor, yourself, standing up to be counted in the cause of a minority group. . . . It made my spirits soar.
>
> Too often, I've found, Lutherans seem hesitant to apply their faith to practical issues, and it's heartwarming to realize that there are exceptions.

Erik wanted to do a story on my participation in the protest. A few weeks later he sent out his own release, accompanied by a  feature story I had written for him: "Into the Lion's Mouth—In Race Relations." I described our experiences and appealed to others to stand up against the lion of racism:

> As one of the few whites who have dared to take a public stand in favor of the Negroes, I have been singled out for abusive treatment by many of the white people, and for praise by others. Were it not for the protecting hand of God, the lives of my wife, my children and myself would likely be in grave danger. Truly we feel a kinship with the man at the circus. Our heads are in the lion's mouth.
>
> A few weeks ago, the rumors were flying thick and fast. Some said that I had been driven out of town, in various states of attire. Others that we were voluntarily moving to a new location. Obviously the rumors were nothing more than wishful thinking on the part of those who started them. Last week we had a large section of our back and side yard plowed up for a garden. Part of it is already planted. We intend to be here to harvest not only our garden, but also the fields which our Lord had in mind when He said, "The harvest truly is plenteous, but the labourers are few; pray ye therefore the Lord of the harvest, that he will send forth labourers into his harvest."

I also offered a rationale for my taking time away from church duties to be involved in such a thing as a bus protest:

> I cannot minister to souls alone. My people also have bodies. "Pie in the sky by and by" may be a fine thing to look forward to. But my people deserve the opportunity to live a decent life in this world, too.

It seemed that the whole world was watching Montgomery, and that exposure provided us a measure of protection we might not otherwise have enjoyed. If the Negroes of Montgomery were mistreated, the story would be carried instantly to the far corners of the globe.

Trinity's church log includes the following entries:

> Jan. 4—Interviewed by local *Time* magazine correspondent—Bill McDonald.
>
> Jan. 6—Interviewed by reporter from *Minneapolis Tribune*—Dick Cleeman, who is working on a series for his paper, called "Dixie Divided."
>
> Jan. 26—Assisted *Life* photographer around town.
>
> Feb. 17—Met with Harold Fey, editor of the *Christian Century*.

Fey was only one of many Christian journalists who paraded through Montgomery, covering the unfolding saga of the American racial revolution.

Another man, a prestigious editor, called me from the airport and asked if I could meet him in a downtown hotel. When I arrived, I found him in the hotel's restaurant, eating his dinner. He proceeded to interview me while he ate, never bothering to offer me so much as a cup of coffee. After about thirty minutes, he thanked me and left for the airport. After that brief encounter, he wrote an article for his publication, suggesting that he had been involved in the Montgomery story.

His actions were duplicated many times in secular press. Everyone wanted to be perceived as "part of the Montgomery story."

Others wanted to be part of the story too, though in a different way. Tom Johnson's column stirred up discussions all over Montgomery. In one white neighborhood the residents delegated one of their number to pay us a call.

We were surely surprised to find an older white man at our door one day. He seemed friendly enough, so we invited him in. Our visitor gave his name and address, then explained the purpose of his visit. "The people in my community have voted that you should leave town," he told us. "For the good of Montgomery, as well as your own good, you must move immediately." We thanked him for his concern for our well-being but assured him that we would be staying.

An even more unfriendly visitor, a police lieutenant, came to our house one day and asked to come in. When he told us he was from Boston, we thought he might be reasonably liberal on racial matters. But our northern visitor was the most racist Montgomery police officer we met. Though I tried to be hospitable, his mean, nasty conversation disturbed Jeannie so much that she left the room.

Because of such incidents, we decided to record conversations with unfriendly visitors. The bulky reel-to-reel tape recorders of those days were hard to hide, but our ever-present baby buggy made a nice hiding place. We were glad none of our visitors were friendly enough to want to look at the "baby."

The visitors and threats prompted other precautionary actions as well. Our living room couch sat across from the picture window, and our older children loved to play in the space behind it, so we turned that into a game. We told Margee and Bobby that anytime we said, "Go hide!" they should quickly get behind the couch. We even held drills. The children loved it. That game could have saved their lives. Both times our house was bombed, the picture window exploded with such force that the wall was peppered with tiny fragments of glass drilled into the plaster.

Montgomery became such a curiosity that a biracial group of graduate sociology students came from Fisk University in Nashville, Tennessee, to study the bus protest as a research project. White students interviewed white people and Negro students, Negroes.

Upon the completion of the study, our Montgomery Improvement Association board invited the students to a special dinner meeting and heard their findings. We found much of the report hilarious: white people in general were bewildered by what was going on, and there was a strong consensus that the commotion was caused by "outside agitators" because "our niggers" wouldn't do anything like this.

Rev. Solomon S. Seay, who was born and raised just a few miles from Montgomery, told me that every time he had ever attempted to challenge the system of segregation and discrimination, he had been accused of being an *outside* agitator.

A significant number of white people placed the blame on that "Nigger King and the nigger-lovin' preacher." More sophisticated interviewees traced the disturbance to a conspiracy of the Communist Party, the National Association for the Advancement of Colored People, and the Lutheran Church.

In the months that followed I began traveling out of state more often. In early February I flew to Columbus, Ohio, to meet with District President Otto Ebert and three national church officials. They wanted to give me an opportunity to talk freely, away from the pressures I would feel in Montgomery. They also showed great concern for our safety. If Jeannie and I felt we were in any jeopardy, they were ready to move us out of town immediately. (We knew all along that we were in danger, but we were not about to move.) When they asked about my violation of state and local laws, I explained that I violated segregation laws practically every time I turned around.

Their final concern was the impact of my involvement and its publicity on my ministry. All four men delighted to hear my reports about Negro people being more receptive to the ministry of the Lutheran Church, a largely unknown denomination to most Negroes. But Negro-missions director Ervin Krebs was most moved when I talked about the number of Negro people who had confessed to me that, before they met us, they believed it was impossible for a white man to be a Christian.

American Missions Director Dale Lechleitner's thoughts were moving in a different direction. He could scarcely hide his glee as he made his final statement, "I'm glad we finally did something before the Catholics did!"

All four men expressed their support. The church log says, "They are with us."

But not long afterward, Lechleitner demonstrated that support in a concrete way. Informed that the insurance company was planning to cancel our fire insurance, he called their national office and announced, "If that policy is canceled, every policy you carry on any Lutheran church in this country will be canceled as well!"

Our insurance remained in effect.

Two-and-a-half weeks later I returned to Columbus, this time to speak at a fund-raising rally for the Montgomery protest. About twelve-hundred people crowded into Union Grove Baptist Church, and they contributed $2,128. I was impressed by this display of generosity and by the outpouring of concern and assistance we were receiving from all over the country.

One man at the meeting was especially impressed with me. After we moved back to Columbus in 1958, Russell Jones told me that he couldn't believe his eyes or his ears that night. Here was a white man, standing in front of an almost totally Negro gathering, saying, "*We* are going to have to find a way to make it *ourselves*. *We* are going to have to reach down into *our* own pockets and pay *our* own money if *we* want *our* freedom movement to succeed."

Jeannie and I felt totally part of the Negro community. It had never occurred to me that there was anything unusual about the pronouns I was using.

Apparently other people almost viewed me as a Negro, as well. I became part of the Columbus Leadership Conference, spearheaded by Russ Jones. The membership included most of the city's black business and professional leaders. At one of our weekly breakfast meetings, the men were debating the membership application of another white pastor who served a black congregation. A sharp division rose over the question of integrating the organization. I stayed out of the debate.

At one point, a supporter of integration said, "Well, Bob Graetz is already a member."

Immediately a man arguing to preserve the racial integrity of the group answered, "That's Graetz! The question is, Shall we admit *white* members to the Columbus Leadership Conference?"

It was another member of that group who gave me the wise counsel that, no matter how hard I tried, I could never truly understand what it was like to be a Negro because I always had the option of walking out.

A few days after the fund-raising rally at Union Grove Church, some Ohio State University students who had attended wrote to me. Part of OSU's United Student Fellowship, they planned to take their spring break in Alabama that year. They wanted to come to Montgomery for one day to see the bus protest in action. As it turned out, Dr. King's boycott trial was going on at the time. So the students observed the trial, saw the car pool in operation, and attended a mass meeting. Our house became their base of operation for the day. Jeannie got quite used to playing hostess to the never-ending parade of visitors to Montgomery.

A more memorable fund-raising trip took place the following May. Four of us, two white and two Negro, drove to Chicago, Illinois, and Anderson, Indiana. My companions were Mrs. Rosa Parks and Rev. Solomon S. Seay, both active participants in the protest, and Rev. Howard Vines, white minister of the Capital Memorial Church of God, an all-white congregation in Montgomery.

We addressed church services in Chicago and spoke at seminaries in both cities. In Anderson we also participated in a Community Prayer Service, their first interracial fund-raising and consciousness-stirring meeting initiated by white people.

On that journey I learned some of the problems Negroes faced as they traveled across the country. Leaving the outskirts of Montgomery, we stopped for gas, and Rev. Seay said, "Let me get out first."

He stepped out of the car. "Where is your rest room, please?" he asked the attendant. Only after he had been directed to a men's room did we order our gasoline. We followed that pattern during the entire trip, refusing to patronize any place that did not have accommodations for Rev. Seay and Mrs. Parks.

Jeannie and I faced the same kind of problem in 1961 when we took two black teenagers, Bill Green and Reynelda Ware, from St. Philips Lutheran Church in Columbus, Ohio, to a Luther League convention in Miami Beach, Florida. Eating, sleeping, and using the bathroom all presented major challenges, especially as we drove into the Deep South.

Because of time pressures, we had to drive all day Sunday. Getting up that morning, we dressed for church, intending to find a worship service on the way. Mid-morning we stopped and asked two young black boys if there was a church in the area. They directed us down a country road, and we found a church building surrounded by cars. The service had already started, but as soon as we stopped the car and opened our doors, magically every window on our side of the church immediately filled with faces—all white!

"Let's get out of here," Bill urged.

None of us objected. We quickly closed the doors and drove away. All morning we watched for a church, but we finally gave up, deciding to change into more comfortable clothes when we stopped for gas.

At the station, Bill went for a key to the rest room while I arranged for our fuel. He came back, looking puzzled. "It says colored men," he said. "What are we going to do?"

"We'll both change our clothes in the colored-men's room, Bill," I responded. And so we did.

As we drove away, Jeannie told us that she left the car before Reynelda and picked up the key to the white-ladies' room, where they both changed. That poor, bewildered attendant probably hoped no one else would show up until after we had cleared out.

What a waste of resources. Sometimes even a small service station would have four restrooms, labeled: White Ladies, Colored Women, White Gentlemen, and Colored Men. Sometimes there were no facilities at all for "colored" people.

Not all such experiences were that carefree, however. Stopping at a rest area along Florida's Sunshine Parkway, we saw quite a few white people standing around. As we got out of the car, we became the center of attention. The angry looks and mumbled conversations around us made us uneasy. When Bill asked what we should do, I suggested that we separate and use the prescribed facilities.

Even that was not enough to satisfy the angry white men watching us. One man, who reminded me of that gorilla deputy sheriff in Montgomery, followed me into the men's room, stood behind me while I took care of my business, and then followed me out. We never did figure out what he thought I might be trying to do.

Eating meals created additional difficulties though we were never threatened. We knew better than to attempt to eat together in a white restaurant. "Colored" establishments opened their doors freely to us.

That same Sunday afternoon, we saw a sign in an obviously white restaurant advertising a Sunday special. When I walked in by myself and asked for four takeout meals, the hostess knew immediately I was a Northerner, so she tried to be as gracious as possible. "Bring the family inside where you can relax and enjoy your food better," she urged. "It's too hot outside."

Meanwhile, one of the other waitresses happened to look out the window and saw who was in our "family." Quickly sidling up to the hostess, she whispered in a voice I was not supposed to hear, "They've got 'colored' out there."

The hostess, still smiling graciously, began spouting orders to the staff to get our meals for us.

Others, who had heard only the original conversation came by and encouraged me to bring the "family" inside. One at a time they received the same whispered message, each time a little more desperate. I could scarcely keep from laughing out loud.

But laugh we did, as we drove away with four of the biggest carry-out meals I had ever seen. They were willing to be generous if only we would stay away.

Actually, Reynelda's skin was so light that many people did not recognize her as a black person. If it had not been for Bill, we might have evaded the segregation laws with no one the wiser.

But on that trip to Chicago in 1956, there was no way to avoid notice. Rev. Seay was one of the darkest men I ever knew. Nobody could mistake his race.

He had a wonderful sense of humor about it. In 1957, after the buses were integrated, the MIA board was making future plans at the home of Mrs. A. W. West. Mrs. West brought out a tray of cups filled with coffee, some with cream, some without. One by one we helped ourselves. One man reached for the last cup but stopped short. "I don't want that black coffee," he quipped. "It'll turn my skin dark."

We all chuckled, but the chuckles turned to guffaws when Rev. Seay took the cup, saying, "Well, it won't hurt me none."

His sense of humor came through again in the fall of 1958 after I had accepted the call to become pastor of St. Philips Lutheran Church in Columbus. A representative of that church, Mr. Clifford Tyree, came down from Columbus to spend some time with us, and I took him to a mass meeting. Cliff sat in the front row while I joined the other ministers on the platform.

Rev. Seay, presiding, started to introduce Cliff. "One of the members of that church in Columbus that is taking the Graetzes away from us," he began, "is with us tonight, sitting right down here in front."

At that moment everyone in the entire balcony rose up as one person, trying to see what Cliff looked like.

Rev. Seay smiled. "Oh, don't worry," he assured them. "He looks just like me."

They all laughed and sat back down.

With his great sense of humor and his constant aura of self-confidence, Rev. Seay was a source of strength to all of us throughout his life. We saw him for the last time in the spring of 1987. Dying of cancer, he was confined to his bed. After a marvelous, laugh-filled visit, mostly reminiscing, it was time for us to leave. When I asked if I could pray with him, Rev. Seay had only one request: "Please ask God to grant me a peaceful passing into my eternal life," he said.

The memory of Rev. Seay's passing brings to mind the beginning of another life. Back in 1956, I was reluctant to be making so many trips out of town, not only because of leaving Jeannie at home alone with Margee and Bobby, but on January 24, before I had taken the first trip, Dianne Elaine Graetz had been born.

What a wonderful baby! From the time she arrived, Dianne was so pleasant and peaceful, sleeping straight through the night from the time she came home, we could scarcely believe it. We needed that kind of a break. The week Dianne was born, I preached or spoke four different times and took part in six meetings, among other activities.

That was a typical week. But God had given us an atypical baby. We always felt that Dianne's pleasant personality was God's special gift, his way of reminding us that he was still in charge, even over the little details of life. We needed that reminder. We did not know it at the time, but our testing had scarcely begun.

*Rev. Bob Graetz with Bobby, Margee, and Dianne,*
*after Dianne's baptism.*

# 6

## THE OPPOSITION ESCALATES

**M**y arrest by the Montgomery County Sheriff was not the only such incident. The authorities detained car pool drivers on various charges in an obvious attempt to hamper our operations. Dr. King himself was picked up by the police, allegedly for driving thirty miles an hour in a 25 MPH zone.

One Montgomery resident suggested a more effective method than arrest for silencing me. His letter was printed in the *Alabama Journal-Montgomery Advertiser* on Sunday, January 15, 1956:

Another John Brown

Editor, the *Advertiser:*

I read the article written by Tom Johnson of the *Advertiser* staff describing the activities of Rev. Robert S. Graetz. While he was sent here to be the pastor of a Negro church on Cleveland Ave., it appears that he spends more time stirring up dissatisfaction among the Negroes than he spends in the pulpit.

I noticed that Graetz hails from Charleston, W. Va. After reading this article I just casually picked up a book from my encyclopedia, flipped it open and by some strange coincidence I read that in 1859, just 96 years ago, in Charleston, Va., another fanatic by the name of John Brown was hanged.

James H. Greene,
Montgomery

The Negro drivers and the new John Brown concerned the white leaders in Montgomery, as the *Advertiser* reported on January 25, 1956:

> Mayor W. A. Gayle, speaking for the City Commission, urged white Montgomerians yesterday to halt the practice of using their automobiles as "taxi services for Negro maids and cooks who work for them."
>
> He said the maids and cooks by boycotting the Montgomery City Lines are "fighting to destroy our social fabric just as much as the Negro radicals who are leading them."
>
> "The Negroes are laughing at white people behind their backs. They think it's very funny and amusing that whites who are opposed to the Negro boycott will act as chauffeurs to Negroes who are boycotting the buses. . . .
>
> "When a white person gives a Negro a single penny for transportation or helps a Negro with his transportation, even if it's a block ride, he is helping the Negro radicals who run the boycott.
>
> "The Negroes have made their own bed and the whites should let them sleep in it."

The mayor also announced that all three of Montgomery's commissioners, including himself, had joined the White Citizens' Council. After the mayor's call to arms, many white housewives received nasty, threatening phone calls and were harassed in other ways.

Later that year, a troublesome letter circulated:

> Dear friend: listed below are a few of the white people who are still hauling their Negro maids. This must be stopped. These people would appreciate a call from you, day or night. Let's let them know how we feel about them hauling Negroes.

The list of names, addresses, and phone numbers of those still providing transportation included some prominent members of Montgomery society.

After the letters were circulated, women reported getting calls from men, mostly after midnight, using profanity and threats of violence. The most frequent question: "Isn't it about time you went to get your nigger maid?" One of the housewives, who protested when awakened by a midnight call, was told, "You ain't heard nothing yet unless you stop hauling your Negro maid."

Some of our opponents did more than talk. On the evening of January 30, a small bomb landed on the porch of Martin and Coretta King's home. Coretta had been visiting with a friend when the two women heard the object land. Not knowing what was happening and not wanting to take any chances, they moved to the back of the house. When the bomb exploded, no one was hurt, and the bomb caused little damage.

Trinity's log says, "Jan. 30—Dr. King's house bombed—police guarded us all night."

Two days later another small bomb was thrown into the yard of Mr. and Mrs. E. D. Nixon, causing little damage.

The wave of anger that swept through the Negro community far overshadowed the bomb explosion. Dr. King's calls for love and nonviolence had not yet filtered into the hearts and souls of most Montgomery Negroes. They only knew that our enemies' violence had risen to a new level, and our leader had been attacked. A large crowd of angry Negro men filled the streets around the King home.

Dr. King had been at a mass meeting, from which he was hurriedly summoned. Onto his front porch crowded Montgomery's three city commissioners, the police chief, and virtually the entire leadership of the city.

Joe Azbell, the *Advertiser's* city editor, described the scene for me. "Dr. King saved our lives," he said. "All of us white people who were there would have been killed by that mob if King had not stopped them."

Seeing that the men in the street were ready to take matters into their own hands, an official asked Martin King to try to calm them.

In his own account of the Montgomery story, *Stride toward Freedom,* King tells what happened next:

> In this atmosphere I walked out to the porch and asked the crowd
> to come to order. In less than a moment there was complete silence.

Quietly I told them that I was all right and that my wife and baby were all right. "Now let's not become panicky," I continued. "If you have weapons, take them home; if you do not have them, please do not seek to get them. We cannot solve this problem through retaliatory violence. We must meet violence with nonviolence. Remember the words of Jesus: 'He who lives by the sword will perish by the sword.'" I then urged them to leave peacefully. "We must love our white brothers," I said, "no matter what they do to us. We must make them know that we love them. Jesus still cries out in words that echo across the centuries: 'Love your enemies; bless them that curse you; pray for them that despitefully use you.' This is what we must live by. We must meet hate with love. Remember," I ended, "if I am stopped, this movement will not stop, because God is with the movement. Go home with this glowing faith and this radiant assurance."

Soon the crowd dispersed. That night that King said "could well have been the darkest night in Montgomery's history" ended peacefully.

After the bombings at the King and Nixon homes, members of Trinity Lutheran became more concerned about *our* well-being. Financial gifts had come to us from people around the country, some earmarked for the congregation's use. Trinity's church council decided to install floodlights at the corners of the parsonage. Perched on the bank, the house really stood out with the floodlights on. The lights, however, did not prevent the bombings in the months that followed.

The church council also decided to hire a night watchman. But the man we hired didn't last long. He spent more time in the tavern across the street than he did watching the house. A second night watchman didn't last much longer than the first. When we discovered he insisted on carrying a gun, we dropped the idea of a night watchman altogether.

But our opponents had other more immediate plans in the works. Early in February a grand jury began reviewing evidence that the Montgomery Improvement Association was engaged in an illegal boycott. On Tuesday, February 21, I was subpoenaed to testify.

Entering the grand jury room reminded me of my encounter with the sheriff and his deputy. Once again I found myself in a closed room surrounded by hostile people. Never in my life had I seen a more vivid picture of anger and hate on men's faces. The one token Negro on the grand jury sat in the corner and never opened his mouth.

Deep fear gripped me—a fear I rarely experienced during the movement. But each time I found myself in such a hostile environment, cut off from my friends, a pall of oppression smothered me. Those times of isolation were the most depressing times of our entire Montgomery experience—not the bombs, nor the threats, nor the nasty phone calls and letters—nothing was as frightening as that feeling of total helplessness.

Any time I left the house to go downtown or head to the airport or drive to another town in Alabama to carry on my ministry, I knew I was leaving my refuge to go into enemy territory. Each time I said good-bye to Jeannie and the children, I knew that this could be the last time in this world that I would see them. We lived each day knowing that our lives, mine especially, might come to a violent end at any moment.

I remember walking home from the courthouse one afternoon following a full day of anxiously waiting to testify. Not realizing how depression had overwhelmed me, I ambled numbly along the rows of commercial buildings and into a white residential neighborhood.

Finally, a few blocks from home, I reached a Negro section. In an instant my spirit changed. I felt as if a heavy load had been removed from me. I was smiling, walking more briskly, believing that the world was a friendly place after all. My feelings transformed the moment I crossed into the Negro neighborhood. I was home again—with my friends!

But I didn't see any friends or friendly faces in the grand jury room the day I testified. Even Mr. E. T. Sinclair, the lone Negro juror, hardly dared to look at me during the proceedings. I am sure he felt helpless. Nothing he said or did was going to make any difference in the outcome.

The morning went more smoothly than I had thought possible in spite of their difficult antagonistic questions. I tried to answer them honestly, though I was considerably less than brave in the presence of such animosity, giving some equivocating responses. Finally it was time for lunch. Unfortunately the grand jury was not quite finished with me, and they told me to come back later.

The evening before, I had missed the mass meeting at St. John AME (African Methodist Episcopal) Church, a black denomination, but I needed to deliver a message to the protest leaders. So I drove to St. John Church and waited in the parsonage next door. As Rev. Abernathy and others came into the front room of the house, reporters followed.

I delivered my message and prepared to leave, but a photographer for one of the local newspapers asked us to pose for him first. The reporter got his picture. I got into trouble.

When the jurors returned for the afternoon session, one of them seemed even more angry than he had been in the morning. "I thought you told us you were not one of the leaders of this boycott," he snarled.

Indeed that morning I had been glad to reveal to them that I was neither an officer nor a board member in the MIA. I did not join the MIA Board of Trustees until the following April 19, and sometime later was promoted to the Board of Directors.

"That's correct," I said. "I'm not one of the leaders."

"Then what about this?" He slammed a copy of the newspaper he had just bought onto the table in front of me. At the top of the front page under a picture of Attorney Fred Gray, Rev. Ralph Abernathy, Rev. U. J. Fields, and me, the caption read: Leaders in Boycott.

"Oh, I can explain that" —

"I'll bet you can!" he snapped. But he never gave me a chance. My interrogation ended.

Later that afternoon the grand jury returned one hundred and fifteen indictments against participants in the bus protest, all charged with violating Alabama's antiboycott law. To the embarrassment of white leaders, however, many of the indictments were faulty. Some defendants had been indicted twice. Rev. A. W. Wilson should have been immune from indictment, as I was, because he had been called to testify before the grand jury. Another man, Mr. Rufus Lewis, one of the top leaders of the movement, was not indicted. The grand jury may have intended to include Mr. Lewis, however; his name appeared on a list they gave to the local papers.

During the next two days, sheriff's deputies were busy arresting all those who had been indicted. But the arrests were like none that Montgomery had ever witnessed. On Wednesday morning, many Negroes who expected to be arrested began turning themselves in at the county jail. After posting bond, they were released immediately. Some of those arrested checked the lists for names of their friends, whom they then called, suggesting that they come on downtown.

The most disappointed people in Montgomery were Negro leaders who were not indicted. One man went to the sheriff and argued with him, trying to convince him that there had been a mistake; he was supposed to be arrested. When everything was finally sorted out, ninety-three people had been indicted, including twenty-six ministers. Three indictments were later dropped when the first trial began.

I was relieved that my appearance before the grand jury had left me immune from indictment. My colleagues talked often about our all going to jail, if necessary. But I firmly declared, "You can go to jail if you want, but leave me out of it. You'll all be together on your side; but I'll be all by myself."

At that time we were still holding mass meetings each Monday and Thursday evening. Since a gathering was already scheduled for Thursday, February 23, the day before the arraignments, a huge crowd thronged into the Negro First Baptist Church that evening.

Not only did the people register support for their arrested leaders, they also decided that the next day, the day of the arraignments, should be a Prayer and Pilgrimage Day. No Negroes would ride in cars, and certainly no one would get on a city bus. I recorded in the log at Trinity: "Prayer and Pilgrimage Day in Montgomery—every member of family walked today." Even Dianne was involved. Jeannie carried her all the way to the doctor's office for her appointment.

On arraignment day, Circuit Court Judge Eugene Carter received not-guilty pleas from the defendants, setting the week of March 19 for all the trials. Evidently the judge anticipated quick guilty verdicts.

Once again I was subpoenaed as a witness for the prosecution. Our defense lawyers asked that the cases be tried one at a time. Dr. King would be the first. In order to clarify the expected appeal, the defense team felt we would be better off having the judge decide the cases alone, though Fred Gray told me, "It would be fun to see if they could put together that many juries."

Joe Azbell and several other reporters were called as prosecution witnesses against Dr. King. Before the trial began, Joe said to me, "They'd better not put me on the stand. If they do, I'll tell them how King saved the lives of all the white leaders of Montgomery." I passed his comment on to Fred Gray.

First the court had to resolve the question of whether the subpoenaed reporters would be allowed to remain in the courtroom during the trial since witnesses are usually excluded from hearing other parts of the trial. Fred announced to the court, "We realize that there is a need for coverage by the local press, so we will agree that Mr. Azbell may be present for the entire proceedings, representing the Montgomery press corps."

Joe was delighted. He was ready to talk.

Not so happy was reporter Bunny Honicker, writing for the *Alabama Journal*. Under the headline, *"Reporter Unable to Tell about Year's Big Story,"* Honicker described the witness room with its "four dust gray walls that may or may not have been ivory-colored in their original state," the "two brownish-yellow windows" that "permit only somber, church-like sunlight to filter in," and the air that was "warm, musty."

Apparently, they were glad to have me and some of my friends around. The March 26 article continued:

## Minister Brings Laugh

Rev. Graetz breaks the silence again. "The most they (the boycott defendants) can get is six months. We're liable to get longer—just staying in here."

Everyone laughs. Both Revs. Graetz and Thrasher along with Negro Rev. A. W. Wilson keep spirits up with their humorous quips from time to time.

For three days I sat in the witness room, waiting to testify. But the prosecution rested its case without calling me. On the fourth and final day the defense called me to the witness stand. To my embarrassment, some of the equivocating statements I had made to the grand jury were read out loud during my cross-examination. When asked to affirm that I had said those things, I could not deny them.

But I knew the time for equivocation was past. After telling the circuit solicitor that I had indeed made the statements he had read, I turned to Judge Eugene Carter and asked for permission to make some additional comments. I trembled as I spoke, but I had to clear my name and proclaim my support of Dr. King.

The trial soon ended. Dr. King's conviction carried a fine of five hundred dollars plus court costs. When our attorneys announced their intention to appeal the conviction, the court decided to postpone the other trials until the process had been completed. As it turned out, they were never held because the subsequent federal court ruling outlawing segregated bus seating made the state court cases moot.

WE REMAINED constantly alert for new forms of harassment, sometimes seeing it where it didn't exist. When I was asked to preach at Talladega College, a Negro school in Talladega, Alabama, Jeannie and I arrived on a Saturday and stayed in a dormitory room. In the middle of the night, banging and clanging sounds echoed through the high-ceilinged hallway outside. Someone must have learned that we had come to Talladega. Jeannie and I listened anxiously, half expecting the attacker to come bursting through the doorway.

Then we heard one of the adults on the floor go out into the hall to see what was happening. Sounds carried well in that old building, so we heard the entire conversation. The culprit, a telephone company employee, apologized, explaining that all the phones in the Talladega exchange had to be changed during the next twenty-four hours. Service representatives had been sent out to public buildings during the night and would be in private homes the next day. All was well.

But not all potential threats had such benign endings. Driving in Montgomery one day, my last task before going home was to drop off some books at the public library. While waiting for the traffic signal to turn green, I saw a passenger in the car ahead turn and look in my direction. Becoming very excited, he began talking to the driver, who also turned to get a look. The first face was unfamiliar, but the second I recognized: Sheriff Mac Sim Butler! I hadn't even noticed the insignia on his car.

The nightmare began. Although the library was just a few feet away on my left, the sheriff's department was not more than fifty yards ahead on the right.

When the light changed, Sheriff Butler raced into his parking lot while I waited to make my left turn. I watched fearfully as the two jumped out of their car and talked to some men standing around. The sheriff kept pointing in my direction. I thought the traffic would never clear up so I could get out of there. Finally, just as I was making my turn, I saw a group of men jump into a civilian car and race out of the parking lot.

By this time my brain was racing as fast as my car. I had already canceled the library stop. Presuming those men had been sent to beat me up, or worse, I just wanted to get away. The street climbed a hill, then leveled off abruptly. Topping the crest of the hill, I watched my pursuers drop out of view. I turned quickly into the first alley I could find.

I dared not head toward home. They would be looking for me there. So I made another right turn, heading back toward the sheriff's office. After driving around downtown Montgomery for a while, I went home by a different route, relieved that I had somehow eluded them. Though I was often followed when I drove out of town, I was never involved in another such "chase."

But another incident was even more frightening.

On Sunday, August 19, 1956, Mrs. Rosa Parks left with our whole family for a week at Highlander Folk School in Monteagle, Tennessee. We were taking part in a workshop on public-school integration. The landmark Supreme Court decision on school integration had been handed down two years earlier.

This was also a badly needed vacation. What a wonderful week it was! There were no demands beyond the workshop's schedule, no phones in our cabin. The program included plenty of time for group singing and other activities our children could enjoy. And we formed many new friendships.

Highlander's policy put all participants on an equal basis, no matter what their rank or importance. All jobs were shared by everyone. One of our most delightful memories of that week was doing the dishes one day with Dr. Benjamin Mays, president of Morehouse College in Atlanta, Georgia, where Dr. King had gone to school. Dr. Mays had been a major influence in King's development.

We went to bed on Friday night, knowing the workshop would end the next morning and we would be on our way back to Montgomery.

But the week ended more abruptly than we had anticipated. Early Saturday morning we heard a knock at our door, summoning me for *New York Post* reporter Ted Poston's long-distance phone call, informing us that our house had been bombed.

By the time I got back to the cabin and told Jeannie what had happened, the entire workshop group had been roused out of bed. Our three-year-old Margee best explained what had happened: "Our house got broke."

After breakfast together, our friends surrounded us with their love and sang with us one of the folk songs of the civil rights movement: "We shall not, we shall not be moved; just like a tree that's planted by the water, we shall not be moved." Then we were on our way.

Montgomery Mayor W. A. Gayle accused us of staging the bombing. The *Alabama Journal* quoted him in its August 25 Final Home edition:

> "This latest 'bombing' follows the usual pattern," Gayle said. "It's a strange coincidence that when interest appears to be lagging in the bus boycott something like this happens.
>
> "It's interesting to note that Rev. Graetz and his family were out of town and the explosion was set off at least 20 feet away from the house at 1110 Cleveland Avenue so that no extensive damage was done.
>
> "We are inclined to wonder if our-of-state contributions to the boycott have been dropping off. Perhaps this is just a publicity stunt to

build up interest of the Negroes in their campaign."

The paper then gave a more rational explanation for the timing of the bombing. Before we left town, I had sent another letter to the members of the all-white Montgomery Ministerial Association, inviting them to a meeting of the Montgomery Council on Human Relations. Dr. King would be speaking on Thursday, August 23. They could hear our side of the story in a nonthreatening atmosphere.

A Baptist minister, however, responded by sending his own letter to the pastors (with a copy to the local papers), warning them not to attend. Not one white minister dared come to the meeting. One white stranger attended, an older man dressed in shabby clothes. Evidently, he felt he needed to "dress down" to be inconspicuous in a Negro meeting. But his attire made him stand out all the more. Everyone assumed he had come to spy.

On August 26, the *Montgomery Advertiser* reported:

> The white minister of a Negro church whose home was damaged by a dynamite blast early yesterday charged Mayor W. A. Gayle with "foolishness" in calling the bombing a "publicity stunt" . . .
>
> The minister said he surmised that the latest violence was brought about by the "same group" responsible for the earlier bombings "or by like-minded persons since it all follows a similar pattern."

Accompanying the article was a picture of me with Margee and Bobby, measuring the bomb hole. The hole was fifteen inches deep and twenty-one inches across. Another picture showed the home of our neighbors, Mr. and Mrs. B. T. Knox, whose windows were also broken by the blast.

The drive from Monteagle back to Montgomery seemed a great deal longer than the trip north had been. We were all tense, not knowing what we would find when we arrived home. Our first look at the broken windows and other damage surprised us. We had expected the house to be in much worse condition. Police had cordoned off the area with ropes to keep the crowds at bay.

We quickly surveyed the damage and checked the house. Unknown to Jeannie and me, Mrs. Parks quietly began sweeping the kitchen and picking up broken dishes.

Soon after our arrival, Mr. Robert Dandridge came walking in, laughing heartily. "You should hear Bobby," he told us. "He's outside here saying, 'Get away, you old bad policeman!'"

Mr. Dandridge had practically adopted Bobby as his own. His only son, also named Robert, had gone to Ohio State University years earlier, but Robert became ill and died. The Dandridges still grieved over their loss, but Mr. Dandridge had found in our young son a kindred spirit to his offspring.

We learned later that Margee had first made the unfriendly remark, with two-year-old Bobby eagerly joining her.

Actually, the officer guarding our front door probably wished he *could* get away. The men posted outside seemed nervous and tense, watching the sea of hostile black faces staring at them.

I went outside and told the police officers we didn't need them anymore. "We want our friends to be able to come freely to our door," I said. Very quickly the ropes came down and our "protection" vanished.

We were glad to see them go. There were signs that someone had gone through our possessions. One of the reasons the mayor and other officials gave for believing the bombing had been a put-up job was their discovery of empty suitcases in one of our closets.

The only thing missing was our personal telephone directory, which caused great concern. That book contained names and numbers of many of our white friends. We were afraid they would suffer when the information got out.

I called the Montgomery FBI office and talked with my friend Woody Draut.

Immediately he asked, "Was our secret number in the book too?"

The thought shocked me, "Yes," I said. Some weeks before, Woody had given me a special number to use when I was passing information along to them, or reporting about problems we were experiencing. Since we assumed that our phone was being tapped regularly, there might be times we would not want listeners to know I was talking with FBI agents.

Now the police knew of our close connection with the FBI. What should we do?

Woody's next comment took my worries away. "Good!" he said. "Now they'll know we're working with you, and they'll be a little more careful."

That evening I made my entry in the church log:

> Aug. 25—House bombed at approximately 3:00 A.M. Front door and numerous windows damaged in addition to windows and doors of houses next door and across street. Bomb landed 43 feet in front of porch; police estimate 2 or 3 sticks of dynamite. No injuries; entire family in Tennessee at the time. God is still Lord in Montgomery, Alabama. Thank God we can put our trust in Him. Psalm 27.

My hometown newspaper, the *Charleston Gazette*, ran a regular feature called "Intercepted Message" on its editorial page. On August 26, the message was addressed to:

Rev. Robert Graetz

Bombing Victim

Montgomery, Alabama

The text:

Dear Preacher:
    This part of the "reasonable solution" the South is always talking about for its racial problems?
                Yours,
                George

Our enemies never allowed us much time to rest. A few days after the bombing, I came under attack again—from a totally unexpected source.

In the early days of the protest movement, I had been critical of our local newspapers, accusing them of being one-sided in their coverage of events. By this time, however, I had come to realize that the local news media were more accurate and fair than most others around the country.

Many people sent us clippings from their own local newspapers. Most slanted their news coverage to make us look good. The few who opposed us were just as biased in the other direction. But the *Montgomery Advertiser,* the *Alabama Journal,* and the Montgomery television stations were the most objective of all. So I had come to trust local reporters and to be very open with them.

In mid-September, a reporter from the *Montgomery Advertiser* called me to ask about rumors that the Montgomery Improvement Association was having trouble maintaining insurance coverage on the cars in our car pool.

"I've heard the same rumors," I said, "but if you want to know anything about that, you'll have to call the MIA and ask someone there."

The reporter pursued the subject with more questions. I acknowledged having heard those things but kept reminding him that I really didn't know anything about it.

On September 17 a front-page article quoted me as saying virtually everything I had said I didn't know.

## THREATENS POOLS OPERATION

### Graetz Says Boycotters Denied Auto Insurance

A "cat and mouse" game between Montgomery insurance men and drivers in the Negro bus boycott pool—a game which threatens the pool's operation—was reported yesterday by a white minister closely associated with the boycott.

The Rev. Robert Graetz, white pastor of the Negro Trinity Lutheran Church, said the "game" has been going since January, with insurance men repeatedly canceling policies on vehicles used in the pool, and owners constantly seeking reinsurance from new sources.

An editorial in the next day's paper took me to task.

### The Rev. Graetz Is Wrong

The Rev. Robert Graetz, the white Lutheran pastor who is active
in the Montgomery bus boycott, is undoubtedly a man of considerable
courage, however misguided some of his efforts may be.

But courage cannot always be equated with wisdom. In his latest
charge of a conspiracy to boycott the boycott by denying liability insurance, Graetz is guilty of gross misstatements of the facts. . . .

Mr. Graetz would be less than human if by now, in his loneliness as
the only white minister in the boycott, he hadn't developed something
of a persecution complex. But in this case he seems to have been mis-
led by his boycott associates.

I called Joe Azbell, the paper's city editor, to tell him what had happened.

Joe cleared his throat. "The paper can't print a retraction or a public
apology, Reverend," he said. "I hope you understand. But I promise
you, I will correct the situation. Please don't take any further public
action on this. Just leave it to me."

I agreed.

Before long, I learned that the offending reporter had been fired.
Apparently the message reached the rest of the Montgomery press corps.
Nothing like that ever happened again.

Another attack on the movement came from an even more unexpected source. On June 11, 1956, Rev. Uriah J. Fields, pastor of the Bell
Street Baptist Church, resigned as secretary of the MIA, charging, "I
can no longer identify myself with a movement in which the many are
exploited by the few." Giving no specifics, he claimed MIA officers were
"misusing money sent from all over the nation."

Actually, his charges reignited my own concerns about the way money
was handled. I had raised several thousand dollars through speeches at
fund-raisers, and each time, after paying for my travel expenses, I turned

everything else over to the MIA.

After one of those trips, however, when I brought the money in to be deposited, someone asked, "Did you keep enough out for yourself?"

I balked. "I never keep any for personal use," I replied. "This money was raised for the movement."

"I know, but the other speakers normally keep an honorarium for themselves out of the money they raised."

I was shocked. I had no idea others were doing that. But I never changed my policy. I always turned in to the MIA everything above expenses.

As I thought it over, however, I reasoned that the other men might be justified in taking something for themselves. Many of them were poorly paid by their congregation. At that time I received a regular salary of $3,100 a year, plus a free parsonage. Other ministers had incomes much lower than mine.

But Reverend Fields's charges turned virtually the entire Negro community against him. Most "colored" people found it impossible to believe that their leaders would do anything seriously wrong. And even if they did, it was totally inappropriate to talk about it in public. Bell Street Baptist voted unanimously to dismiss him. Fields became a total outcast.

But on the following Monday evening, Dr. King stood before a large crowd at the regular mass meeting and talked about love and forgiveness. "Reverend Fields is back here now," he said, "and in a minute I'm going to bring him out. I want you to forgive him and accept him back into your fellowship."

When Fields came to the lectern, he looked to me like a broken and humbled man. Though he apologized and retracted the charges he had made, he stopped short of saying that his original statement had been totally false. His relationship with the Montgomery Negro community was never the same. Ironically, the church he pastored, Bell Street Baptist, was one of the bombing targets the following January 10. Fields was replaced as secretary of the MIA. Later still I was elected to that same post.

My election as MIA secretary resulted from internal politics which the masses did not know existed. After my "promotion" from the board of trustees to the board of directors, I discovered quickly that MIA leadership divided into two groups with differing dreams for the future. Though virtual unanimity reigned in most decisions about running the protest, sharp differences arose as we contemplated future activities.

One group, mostly clergy, wanted to focus on largely ceremonial goals, such as integrating airport facilities.

The other, smaller faction, nonclergy except for me, pressed for changes that would affect the masses. Though the clergy, the natural leaders in this church movement, attracted most of the spotlight, the lay participants included some of the most courageous and hard-working people in the Negro community:

Mr. E. D. Nixon, a leader in the Pullman car porters union and president of the Alabama chapter of the NAACP, spent his entire life fighting racial discrimination and prejudice, often at great personal risk.

Mr. Rufus Lewis, a local businessman, headed up our voter-registration campaign and became one of the most effective leaders in the MIA. Attorney Fred Gray and his brother Tom, another local businessman, worked hard in the group as well. They were close coworkers and among our dearest friends.

When the nonclergy group noticed that most major decisions were made by the totally clergy executive committee, they nominated me to the recently vacated position of secretary. Because I was clergy, and the sole white board member, they hoped the other clergy members would not object.

I won the election, but then the executive committee stopped meeting. Decisions were now made informally, outside of the board altogether. The only time Dr. King called me into his office during that period, he wanted to know why I was fighting him.

"I'm not fighting you, Martin," I assured him. "The others and I simply support positive actions that can bring the greatest benefit to the largest number of people."

Martin ultimately realized there was no personal struggle between the two of us.

In spite of all the problems we faced, Jeannie and I could not feel sorry for ourselves. We knew that the "colored" people in our church and our community had suffered far more than we had, and for many more years. One of our members, for example, was fired from her job simply because she belonged to the church where I was the pastor.

During the protest, many people proved their willingness to suffer, particularly if it would help someone else. At a mass meeting one evening, a minister told about seeing an old woman walking along, far from any Negro community. As he pulled over to pick her up, he said, "Sister, aren't your feet tired?"

"Mister," she said, "for all these years my feet's been resting, but my soul's been tired. Now my feets is tired, but my soul's resting."

Another old woman walked up to a dispatch station one day to get a ride to work. the dispatcher shook his head sadly. "Sister, you are just a little bit too late," he said. "The last station wagon left a few minutes ago, and there won't be any more cars in here for a long time. Look," he continued, "everybody knows you're part of the movement. It's a bad day, and you have a long way to go. Why don't you just go ahead and ride the bus today."

The old lady drew herself up to her full height and looked down her nose at the man. "Son, I'm not doing this for myself," she said. "I've got a little grandson at home. I want him to be able to get on that bus, pay his dime, and take his seat!" With that she turned and began walking to work, several miles away.

One other incident involved us indirectly. One morning in early August 1956, two dummies, one black and one white, hung on Court Square in downtown Montgomery. The black dummy wore the label, *NAACP*. The white one bore the words, *"I talked integration."* Clearly we were meddling in an explosive issue. People had strong feelings. They took this quite seriously. And some of them would have been happy to see *me* hanging there on Court Square instead of that dummy.

But we were there because God had brought us there. And we were convinced that we were carrying out the task God had given us to do. So we were not about to leave or to change what we were doing. We identified with the civil rights folk song, "Ain't gonna let nobody turn me 'round. I'm heading for the Freedom Land."

# 7

## A CIRCLE OF LOVE

People in Montgomery either hated us or loved us. Few showed indifference. I walked into a shop one day to rent a post-hole-digger. As the owner filled out the rental form, he said to me, "That's G-r-a-e-t-z, isn't it?"

"Yes," I answered. "How did you know?"

"Oh, you're famous," he smiled broadly.

"Do you mean famous or notorious?" I asked.

"I said famous," he replied, "but you can pick whichever one you like."

People often said we had courage. I can't speak for the rest of the people in Montgomery, but there were times when I was scared to death! We began to define courage as doing what needed to be done, even when you were afraid.

Indeed, during the first weeks of the protest, we experienced real terror, and once the threatening phone calls and vandalism began, our apprehensions fed on themselves. We expected bad things to happen. One evening I walked across the lawn to work in the church office. Entering the door closest to the house, I strolled through the dark building. The light switch was by the entrance on the north side, but that was farther away. Knowing the layout of the sanctuary, I could confidently walk through the building in the dark.

But that night my confidence did me in. Reaching the front of the nave, I turned left for a few steps, then right to go into my office. I must have turned one step too soon. I walked briskly right into the rough-plastered wall. Stunned, I stood there for a few seconds, trying to figure out what had happened to me. I felt dizzy, and blood began to run down my forehead. I headed home.

But I hadn't thought of the impact my appearance would have on Jeannie. When I walked through the door, she "knew" that the Klan had gotten me.

I was much more careful after that.

Actually, we were more concerned about our children's well-being than our own. Margee and Bobby loved to play in the big field behind our house, a safe place in center of the block, entirely surrounded by Negro families.

Not content with making threats against the two of us, our anonymous callers knew where we were most vulnerable. A voice on the phone would say, "Do you know where those little fair-haired children are? I saw them out in the field earlier, but they're not there anymore."

We didn't like keeping the children confined. Before the phone calls began, we could allow them to play freely in the front yard, especially around the fig tree, one of their favorite playhouses. But after their lives were threatened, we dared not be so relaxed.

As Jeannie and I discussed the dangers facing us, we knew we were putting our children's lives in jeopardy also. But we soon realized that we would have to entrust their safety to the Lord. He could protect them; we could not.

Jeannie's most anxious moments came when I was out of town. It was not easy being alone with the children when the nasty, threatening phone calls came in. They never really stopped.

One day in January 1956, when I was gone, a young Catholic priest from St. Jude's dropped by to talk. "I was born in the South," he told Jeannie. "I know the terrible things these people are capable of. It's not safe for you to remain in Montgomery," he warned.

By the time he left, Jeannie was terrified. Immediately she called our good friend Bob Hughes and asked him to come over.

It was a real act of courage for our white friends to come to our house. We were always under surveillance, so no one could visit us undetected unless they sneaked in the back way. But that day, parking his car down the street away from our house, Bob came straight to the front door. As they talked, Jeannie poured out all her fears.

Bob told me later that he felt terribly inadequate, fishing for something to say to comfort Jeannie. Finally, he said, "Jeannie, just remember that God is in charge here in Montgomery the same as he is everywhere else."

Though not profound, those words changed our lives.

Jeannie could hardly wait to tell me about it when I got home later that evening. She was bubbling over, definitely not the same fearful person I had said good-bye to the day before.

Describing her experience later, Jeannie said, "It was just a reminder of something we already knew, but it was as if God had opened another door of understanding. That truth expanded within me, and I wanted to shout and praise the Lord. The fear melted away. After that reminder, I felt Jesus's hand on mine as I took the garbage out to the trash can at night or when Bob went over to the church at night. I no longer looked fearfully around or started at every strange sound. I felt a 'circle of love' surrounding us."

Jeannie was at peace, and as she described her experience, my worries and fears lifted from me as well. We felt glorious. Everything was all right. God was in charge of our lives!

Our enemies were everywhere. They hated us and did not slacken their determination to harm us. But God's circle of love, made up of our white and Negro friends who stood by us, never allowed us to feel alone.

Our entire outlook changed. We became bolder than ever. The phone calls, no longer a threat, became a challenge. We knew that even if someone hurt us, God had promised that all things would work out for good to those who love him. We trusted him totally.

Jeannie and I repeatedly turned to Psalm 27 also, which begins, "The Lord is my light and my salvation; whom shall I fear? The Lord is the strength of my life; of whom shall I be afraid? When the wicked, even mine enemies and my foes, came upon me to eat up my flesh, they stumbled and fell. Though an host should encamp against me, my heart shall not fear." We found great strength in that.

Leaving the courthouse one day, I went out through the side door. A white man followed and stopped me at the top of the metal stairway. With his face inches from mine, he called me insulting names and told me the terrible things he was going to do to me.

My heart pounded. He seemed prepared to carry out his threats. There was no one else around to stop him, and though he was bigger than I am, I felt no panic, no terror. Bracing myself for his attack, I looked him straight in the eye.

But the man ran out of words. He turned and stormed down the stairs without ever touching me. Apparently, he intended only to give me a good scare. Now he was mad because he hadn't succeeded.

Another time, a neighbor from the Cleveland Court Apartments came to our back door. Someone had called her from downtown to say that the Ku Klux Klan was gathering on a downtown street, preparing to come out to our house. Since everyone assumed our phone was tapped, he had called our neighbor and asked her to alert us.

We looked out the picture window in the front room. Sure enough, there was a line of cars parked on the street, each filled with several white men.

I turned to Jeannie. "If they came to see us," I said, "we ought to let them see us."

She agreed. We walked out the front door and stood in front of our house while our neighbor waited fearfully inside. Eventually the KKK must have decided they had failed in their attempt to scare us. They drove away.

One day the KKK staged a massive, public show of strength to convince the "niggers" that white people were still in charge. On the chosen Saturday the downtown streets of Montgomery filled with robed men, but most black people ignored them. Shopkeepers chased them away, figuring they were bad for business.

A *Montgomery Advertiser* photographer captured the spirit of the day with a prize-winning photo. A small black boy perched on a fire hydrant looking utterly unconcerned as he watched a group of robed white men pass by.

The fear was gone!

Though there was a new spirit among the Negroes of Montgomery, a new freedom from the oppressing fear that had immobilized them for generations, not everyone had adjusted to the pressures. Most Negroes had lived their entire lives under horrendous white domination; they had not yet experienced God's deliverance from fear.

Our release from the fear's bondage enabled us finally to let our hair down and romp with our children. To see us at home, observers would never suspect that we were in the middle of a major civil rights battle.

One evening we had watermelon for dessert. Jeannie and I often enjoyed pinching watermelon seeds at each other at picnics, and we encouraged the children to join in the mischief. But this night we were not outside at a picnic. We were in our kitchen. Nevertheless, the seeds began flying and we squealed in fun.

When our members visited us in the parsonage, they often used the back door, primarily because it was closer. A few of them, probably reckoning that the building belonged to them anyway, didn't bother to knock when they came in. Mrs. Alice Wilburn, for example, in spite of the fact that she was very proper and very much a lady, usually just walked right in.

As she entered the kitchen door that day, the seeds were flying in every direction, sticking to the ceiling and the walls, hanging from our faces and clothes. But Mrs. Wilburn, proper lady that she was, never saw a thing. She stated her business and quickly made her exit. Maybe she realized that if she had stayed any longer, we could not have kept our laughter bottled up. We would have exploded.

Many people did special things to buoy our spirits. On one occasion, Bob Hughes asked me to help him host a distinguished visitor from India. Mr. H. C. Heda, a member of India's Parliament, was making an official tour of our country. Interested in social change, he wanted to learn all he could about the bus protest. We chatted some, and then I asked Mr. Heda if he would like to attend a mass meeting with Bob and me that evening at a church not far from our house.

He agreed, but it was already late afternoon. Mr. Heda would need something to eat before we went. Our schedule was very tight, but I called Jeannie to see if she could fix dinner for us, reminding her that

Mr. Heda, a Hindu, did not eat meat and that Bob had ulcers. She gave me a short list of items to pick up at the grocery store and said to come on.

The meal was exceptional! And Mr. Heda marveled at the fact that Jeannie and I, who belonged to the white "caste," had chosen to throw in our lot with Negroes, the counterpart, it seemed to him, of India's untouchables.

After dinner, on the way to Holt Street Baptist Church, Mr. Heda explained that he could not speak at the meeting. Because he was representing his government, he dared not take sides on a political issue. But he agreed to bring a greeting. I explained the situation to the minister presiding that evening, and we took our seats on the platform.

The meeting began with hymns and prayers and "rousements," a pep-talk sermon before the main speaker. By the time he rose to speak, Mr. Heda had caught the spirit of the movement. He began with a greeting and an explanation of why he could not say more. Then, catching us all off guard, he moved into a rousing speech comparing the boycott with Gandhi's movement in India. His encouragement spurred us on.

On other occasions, out-of-town reporters gave us a lift. Lee Griggs, a photographer for *Life* magazine, wanted to get some group pictures of the station wagons in our carpool. The heaviest use of the vehicles came in the morning and evening as people traveled to and from work. During the middle of the day, private autos met most of the needs. So we arranged for all the station wagons to be brought to the field behind our house about noon.

For an hour or longer, Lee Griggs perched at the top of a tall step ladder and called down instructions about how he wanted the cars to line up. He shot them in every possible configuration. By the time he was finished, the drivers were becoming nervous about getting to their routes on time. But Lee got what he wanted. The following issue of *Life* magazine carried his pictures, including a magnificent full-page shot of the station wagons lined up in our field. As a surprise bonus for our family, at one side of the picture stood two small children watching the proceedings—Margee and Bobby.

*Station wagons of the car pool, lined up behind parsonage for* Life *magazine photographer Lee Griggs, 1956.*

Another delightful visitor had no connection whatsoever with the bus protest. One day an old white man showed up at our door, asking for food. He looked tired. His clothes and body were dirty. But his most remarkable feature was his totally white hair and full white beard. The children knew in a moment that Santa Claus had come to visit. We brought him in and Jeannie fixed him some food. A stranger from out of town, he knew nothing about who we were, and he didn't care. He may not have even known about the boycott.

Unemployed and nearly penniless, he was wandering around the countryside, looking for help and, hopefully, a job. Our guest happily accepted our offer to stay with us until he got settled. Jeannie washed his clothes, and somewhere we found some more clothing for him.

The children thoroughly enjoyed their visit with Santa. He hadn't carried a sack of toys into our house. In fact, he owned hardly a thing. But he gave them the most precious gift of all—himself. He held them on his lap and talked and played with them. He was a gift to all of us. But soon our Santa moved on. Rested and clean, he felt better and wanted to look for work.

We never saw him again. But a few weeks later a picture of our Santa Claus appeared on the cover of the Sunday paper's magazine section. According to the story inside, this man had wandered into a local greenhouse and asked for a job. It turned out that he was a highly skilled horticulturist. The owners delighted in their new staff member. Santa had found a home.

Thanks to Jeannie's gift for hospitality, our own home became a national and international visitors' center. Reporters, church officials, and the merely curious came from everywhere. Quite a few of them accepted our offer of a place to stay. I especially remember Mr. Kaj Erik Lindqvist, Secretary of the Danish Inter-Church Aid Committee in Copenhagen. During his stay, he tried hard to teach me how to say *Copenhagen* as the Danes did. I never succeeded. Kaj was one of the few people who ever sent me a copy of the story he wrote after he got back home. Of course, it was written in Danish.

Another visitor came to our door one day, not long after the protest began, introducing himself as Special Agent Woodrow E. Draut, Federal Bureau of Investigation. Woody was white, fairly young, and quite likable. He explained that the FBI was interested in what we were doing and that he would be in touch with us on a regular basis. We didn't realize at the time that the FBI had already done a thorough background check on both Jeannie and me.

One day Woody said to Jeannie, "Your dad certainly enjoys a fine reputation back in Pennsylvania. Everyone in the area speaks highly of him." They had even checked up on our families!

We ourselves came under careful scrutiny by the FBI. Their confidential records, which we obtained years later, described us as "loyal and patriotic" with "no criminal record" and "no domestic difficulties." One report says, "Rev. Graetz is a man of extraordinary courage and devotion to his duty as a minister, and as a friend of the Negro." Agents were alerted that they "should at no time speak of Negroes in general in any but a respectful and sympathetic manner, in the presence of Rev. Graetz."

Our relationship with the FBI was most positive. We became good friends with Woody and his wife, occasionally going to their house for a picnic. More important, the agents in the Montgomery office consistently supported and helped us during the bus protest. Whenever useful information came to their attention, they would pass it along to us.

The FBI, of course, had their own reasons for maintaining a good relationship with us. Because of their great concern that the Communist Party or some other subversive group would infiltrate our ranks, they counted on us to inform them of any significant developments.

Though many tried, there is no evidence that any such subversive organization succeeded in breaking into the MIA. While in Chicago to speak at a fund-raising rally, Mr. E. D. Nixon was presented with the keys to a new station wagon for our carpool. As Mr. Nixon was driving the car back to Montgomery, someone discovered the donor group's name on the attorney general's list of subversive organizations. We did not dare to accept the gift. When word reached Mr. Nixon en route, he parked the car, flew home, and mailed the keys back to Chicago.

Another time, Woody called to let me know that the Socialist Workers Party had given one of our ministers a supply of their news publication's current edition because it contained an article about Montgomery. The minister was planning to pass them out at the mass meeting that night.

I manufactured an excuse to drop by to see him. During our conversation, the pastor gave me a copy of the newspaper. But after I explained the nature of the organization that had published it, he burned the papers.

Getting calls from Woody made me feel like I was part of a spy movie. Since we dared not say much over the phone, he and I met in all sorts of places to exchange information. One day he instructed me to come to a downtown business building, take the elevator to the third floor, then follow a passageway that led into the hotel next door. No one should know I had entered the hotel.

Apparently, Woody had arranged a series of meetings in this room. When I entered, he was emptying the contents of an ash tray into an envelope and sealing it. "The man who is coming in next smokes the same brand as the last man," he explained, "and they know each other. Since it's an unusual brand, he might figure out who was here."

Although Jeannie and I enjoyed befriending guests who came into our home, our hospitality sometimes got us into more trouble. One couple came into town and asked to stay with us for a while. They were engaged in a ministry of brotherhood, helping people to come together across racial lines. We were delighted to receive them, but the relationship soon soured.

They did not ask for sleeping accommodations, because their van was equipped as a camper. But that was part of the problem. The sides of the van were covered with huge brotherhood symbols, a white hand clasping a black hand. We attracted enough attention already. We didn't need to inflame the anger of our white neighbors.

Meals presented another problem. We usually ate a simple breakfast. But on their first morning with us, our visitors came inside to eat, and as the man sat down, a look of disgust crossed his face. "Well," he said, "cereal, toast, juice, coffee. I guess that's enough breakfast for anyone."

Our apprehension about our guests deepened as they described their patterns for survival. When they needed fuel for their van, they would drive into a service station and ask to have the tank filled. When the attendant asked for his money, they would request that the gas be considered a donation to their ministry. Invariably, the attendant would refuse, but when the long discussion threatened to keep other customers from the pumps, he would order them to leave and never come back. The couple knew there were plenty of other stations around to meet their needs.

When it became obvious that our increasingly unwelcome guests intended to make our address their semi-permanent location, we groped for a plan to get them to leave. Finally, in desperation, *we* decided to leave town. We packed suitcases and loaded the car.

"We would be happy to stay and take care of the house while you're gone," they assured us.

I don't remember how we convinced them, but we firmly refused their offer. We drove out of town, had a picnic, and a much-needed outing, then drove back home again that evening. The driveway was empty. We had succeeded.

With all the wonderful people around us, even an experience like that could not dampen our spirits. As Jeannie said, we knew we were surrounded by a circle of love.

Chief among those who demonstrated love was Martin Luther King, Jr., the "Apostle of Love" in Montgomery. Martin and Coretta arrived in Montgomery only a few months before we did. We were all young and just out of school. Martin was still twenty-six; I was twenty-seven. Most of the leaders of the movement were in their twenties and filled with youthful idealism. Martin's early life experiences and the example set by his parents and grandparents had taught him that he must never yield to the oppression of racial discrimination. I was a more recent "convert," still riding the crest of enthusiasm generated by my own race-relations conversion.

But Dr. King placed in our hands the tools we would use so effectively in our movement, tools he himself had borrowed from Jesus, Gandhi, and Thoreau, tools of love and nonviolent resistance.

Aside from the fact that such weapons had a strong biblical foundation, there was a practical side as well. Many times Dr. King reminded the Negro people of Montgomery never to use guns and other weapons of violence. The white community was much more heavily armed; they also had the police department at their disposal.

Nor should we rely on economic pressure alone, he said, even though that was the major impact of our protest. Montgomery's Negroes were too poor. They could not possibly win an economic war.

We were left with the weapons Jesus gave us: "Love your enemies, bless them that curse you, do good to them that hate you, and pray for them which despitefully use you, and persecute you." The training in those weapons was not easy. Mistreatment on the buses alone was sufficient to incite the Negroes' anger, besides all the other ways racial oppression had made their lives miserable.

During the first few days of the protest movement, shots were fired at a few of the buses, and there were other expressions of hostility. But little by little, other leaders of the movement echoed the message of love Dr. King preached. And little by little that message seeped into the hearts and lives of the Negro people of Montgomery.

When Negroes said they had thought it was not possible for a white person to be a Christian, they based their observation on their own experiences as well as the centuries-long history of their people. Virtually everything negative in their lives could be traced to whites. Now they were being told to love the very ones who had made them miserable. And they were agreeing to it! These impoverished, downtrodden "colored" people were learning that in the very act of loving their enemies, they were gaining a measure of control over them.

Whites knew how to handle Negroes who were servile. They dealt skillfully with "uppity niggers" who refused to stay in "their place." But whites did not know how to respond to Negroes who laughed when they were threatened and harassed, who rejoiced when they were arrested, and who answered with words of love when assaulted by words of hate. There was no defense against the weapon of love.

I was proud to have had a small symbolic role in that response. When Dr. King was on trial for breaking Alabama's boycott law, I proposed that we all wear white crosses on our lapels, reading "Father, forgive them."

Dr. King's philosophy of love and nonviolence found support in other areas of the country as well. Two men from New York encouraged Martin to make that philosophy the keystone of our movement: Bayard Rustin, a black man, had so strongly committed himself to pacifism that he spent time in jail during World War II. He chose incarceration over any type of participation with a militarist system. Glenn Smiley, a white man, served as National Field Secretary for the Fellowship of Reconciliation, a pacifist organization.

Even at that time, few people fully realized the role that Glenn and Bayard played in the Montgomery protest. Both men carefully avoided the limelight. Though Glenn had many close contacts with Martin, he rarely talked about what they discussed or what influence he may have had over Martin.

Dr. Martin Luther King, of course, needed little influencing. A theologian, philosopher, scholar, orator, and mystic, he was the most remarkable man I ever knew, a man to whom a long list of superlatives applied.

I am amazed that I was not more in awe of Martin from the beginning. A typical recent graduate from a Lutheran seminary, on those rare occasions we had time to talk, I often engaged this Baptist preacher in theological debate.

Of all Martin's outstanding talents, his preaching ability impressed me most. Well-read scholar and accomplished orator that he was, Dr. King could not only make a congregation of uneducated maids and day laborers understand him, but he could also draw them up to his level.

Never condescending, King inspired his listeners to become more than they had ever been before. No wonder they called him Moses. "Colored" people were living in the bondage of slavery, held in captivity by white oppression. God clearly promised that someday they would be free—the message of their beloved Negro spirituals.

This new Moses, sent from God, stood before them declaring that their "someday" was at hand. He pointed the way through the wilderness into the Promised Land. The Negro people of Montgomery had no illusions that they would be freed from all of their shackles instantly. But they were heading for "the Freedom Land." And nobody was going to "turn them 'round." Victory filled the air.

# 8

## VICTORY

Victory in our struggle would not come without a price. But the spirit of that old woman who walked so that her grandson could ride the bus with dignity, characterized the entire Negro community. So we pressed on.

On December 5, 1955, the only demands made of the city administration and the bus company were better treatment of Negro passengers, a more equitable system of enforcing segregation, and a handful of jobs for Negro drivers. In retrospect it was the mildest set of demands one could imagine. But in the "Heart of Dixie" in the mid-1950s, our requests were nothing short of revolutionary. Whites knew that any breach in the wall of segregation could crumble the entire structure.

Negotiations between protest leaders and the city and bus company officials proved mostly a waste of time. Dr. King and others still held out hope for some kind of compromise, but reality imposed itself upon us.

The bombings of the King and Nixon homes had been isolated events. But if questions remained about the white leaders' determination to destroy our movement, the grand jury indictments quickly removed all doubt.

In order to attack the legal underpinnings of segregation, the movement leadership decided to appeal the conviction of Mrs. Parks. But Attorney Gray and our other lawyers realized *that* victory route might take years. The Negroes' determination might give out before we reached our goal.

The federal court system seemed a better prospect because a year and a half earlier, the U.S. Supreme Court had ruled school segregation unconstitutional. So on February 1, 1956, Fred Gray filed suit in federal district court challenging the laws regarding segregation in public transportation. He represented five women, two of whom had been arrested for violating those laws.

One of the five withdrew her name a day later, claiming she had not known what she was signing. There were strong indications, however, that she had been pressured into withdrawing.

The Montgomery County Grand Jury brought an indictment against Attorney Gray for illegally representing the woman who had withdrawn. But the county grand jury had no jurisdiction over a federal suit.

Montgomery's draft board changed Gray's classification from 4-D (reflecting his position as a part-time pastor) to 1-A, making it likely that he would be drafted. The National Selective Service board foiled that conspiracy, however, ordering the local board to return Gray to his previous status.

The federal suit challenged both Montgomery and Alabama bus segregation laws. Because a state statute was involved, federal law required that a three-judge panel hear the case. About a month later, the three judges were named: Richard T. Rives, Seybourn H. Lynne, and Frank M. Johnson, Jr. (in whose court the suit had been filed). All were native Alabamians.

At 9:00 A.M. on May 11, the hearing began on the suit now known as *Browder v. Gayle*. By early afternoon, the testimony and the arguments had been completed. But while the Negro people waited weeks for a decision, they continued to walk and share rides, remaining off the city buses. They had little choice. After the first week of protest, the lack of riders caused bus company officials to cancel routes that went into Negro communities.

Finally, on June 5, exactly six months after the Montgomery protest began, the three-judge panel issued its ruling. In a 2-to-1 decision, the judges declared, "There is now no rational basis upon which the separate but equal doctrine can be validly applied to public carrier transportation in Montgomery or in Alabama."

They gave the litigants two weeks to offer suggestions for implementing their decision. The plaintiffs' attorneys asked for an immediate end to segregation. Defendants wanted to maintain the status quo until they had a chance to appeal the decision.

In spite of the judges' decision, bus segregation laws continued to be enforced. So on June 19 the same panel of judges issued an injunction to end segregated transportation in Montgomery. The injunction, however, was not scheduled to go into effect for ten days, giving defendants an opportunity to appeal the decision to the U. S. Supreme Court. They did—on June 29, the last day they could do so. The suspension of the injunction continued until the appeal could be heard, in October at the earliest.

Nothing had changed in the day-to-day lives of Montgomery's Negroes, yet everything was different. We had won! The months of sacrifice, tired feet, arrests, harassments—even the bombings—had all been worth it.

But the battles were not over yet. The city secured an injunction against the MIA car pool. On November 13 Judge Eugene Carter ordered its operations to cease.

City officials should have known better than to launch another attack on the Negro movement. Every time they did, they revitalized our determination to continue, whatever the cost. And every attack led to more publicity and a new outpouring of gifts to the movement.

The mayor and his cohorts had scarcely a moment to enjoy their victory. Before Judge Carter issued his injunction, the big news reached Montgomery: The U.S. Supreme Court had not even bothered to hear arguments on the city's appeal. Their terse ruling stated: "The motion to affirm is granted and the judgment is affirmed." In the courtroom that day, a reporter handed Dr. King a copy of the Associated Press news release. It read, "The United States Supreme Court today affirmed a decision of a special three-judge U.S. District Court in declaring Alabama's state and local laws requiring segregation on buses unconstitutional."

In *Stride toward Freedom* Dr. King described his feelings when he received the news: "At this moment my heart began to throb with an inexpressible joy. The darkest hour of our struggle had indeed proved to be the first hour of victory."

A Negro bystander said, "God Almighty has spoken from Washington, D.C."

The following day was a busy one for all of us. The log at Trinity Lutheran lists three key entries:

> M.I.A. Executive Board—Special session to consider Supreme Court verdict of November 13, outlawing bus segregation
> Mass Meeting at Hutchinson Street Baptist Church
> Mass Meeting at Holt Street Baptist Church

We thought the Supreme Court's decision would go into effect within a few days, so the injunction against the car pool would not be too difficult to bear. But the law called for a twenty-five day waiting period to allow the losing party time to request a rehearing. We used the waiting time most effectively.

The city did indeed appeal the decision. And the MIA petitioned for an immediate injunction against the segregation laws in order that the buses might be integrated at once. Our request was denied.

Meanwhile, the MIA drew up an informal plan for people to share rides for the next few days. Many people went back to walking. This close to final victory, our people were not about to give up. They had been sacrificing their convenience for over eleven months. A few more days of walking would not be too great a price.

We intensified preparations for returning to the buses. On November 13 the MIA Board recommended that the Negro citizens of Montgomery officially end the bus protest and reboard the buses as soon as the court's injunction had been put into effect. In the two mass meetings that evening, an estimated eight thousand Negroes voted unanimously to accept the recommendation.

Those meetings bubbled over with enthusiasm. Victory radiated from the people's faces and in their demeanor. Rev. Abernathy presided. He asked me to read the Bible's "Love Chapter," 1 Corinthians 13. "Read it like you've never read it before," he said. "Put everything into it." His advice was hardly needed. We were all intoxicated with joy.

At the appropriate time Abernathy announced, "Our Scripture to-night will be read by the Reverend Robert Graetz, pastor of Trinity Lutheran Church." The crowd responded with thunderous applause such as I had never received before.

A reporter near Rev. Abernathy turned to him. "Isn't that a little peculiar, applauding the Scripture?" he asked.

Ralph smiled at him and answered simply, "We are a peculiar people."

I began reading. "Though I speak with the tongues of men and of angels, and have not charity, I am become as sounding brass, or a tin-kling cymbal . . . Charity suffereth long, and is kind; charity envieth not; charity vaunteth not itself, is not puffed up . . . Beareth all things, believeth all things, hopeth all things, endureth all things."

Moving through the passage, I knew the congregation was totally with me. The words described what they had been demonstrating for nearly a year. Never before in their lives had they experienced this deeper meaning of Christian love, especially Jesus's command, "Love your en-emies."

Near the end of the chapter, the crowd once more erupted in ap-plause, as loud as before. Suddenly it dawned on me that this new round of applause was a response to the words I had just read: "When I was a child, I spake as a child, I understood as a child, I thought as a child: but when I became a man, I put away childish things."

The Negro people of Montgomery had achieved adulthood. They had put away childish things. They had earned the right to stand side by side with white people in making the decisions that would affect the lives of all people, regardless of race.

That was the real victory. No court decision, no change in practices or regulations would have made any real difference in Montgomery, Alabama, if the Negro people themselves had not changed. They needed to recognize their own value as human beings. Only then could they step forward and appropriate the legal victory they had won. The real victory, which would begin the slow but inexorable alteration of the South's social life, had been accomplished in the hearts of the black people of Montgomery. That victory would not be denied.

White people couldn't understand the changes that had taken place. Again and again I had heard the refrain: "Our niggers wouldn't act like this!" Indeed they had never seen "their niggers" demonstrate such self-confidence.

Early in the protest, a group of teenage boys stood on a corner watching empty buses roll by. A police car pulled up. "What are you boys doing here?" one of the officers shouted. "I want you all to get away from this corner!"

One of the teenagers calmly walked over to the patrol car. "Mister," he said, "I ain't done nothin'. I ain't going' nowhere. I'm going to stand where I damn am!" The befuddled officers drove away.

Besides encouraging a spirit of love and self-worth, we also used the waiting time for instruction. The MIA did not want anyone to reboard the buses without being trained to accept any violence or insults they might encounter.

Mass meetings became training sessions. Participants played the roles of bus driver, white and Negro passengers, and police officers in various scenarios involving physical and verbal abuse. Glenn Smiley and other Fellowship of Reconciliation members helped us teach the Negroes of Montgomery, a few at a time, how to put the nonviolence philosophy into practice.

We told our people that no one should get back onto a city bus without the training. Furthermore, we asked each person to take a pledge to remain nonviolent, regardless of how badly he or she might be treated. As the weeks went by, we built a cadre of committed people, ready and waiting for the day we would return to the buses.

As the first anniversary of the bus protest approached, we celebrated with a week-long Institute on Nonviolence and Social Change, with the theme, "Gandhi in America." Speakers included such notables as author Lillian Smith and newspaper reporter Carl Rowan, as well as Dr. Martin Luther King, Jr., and Rev. Glenn Smiley. Mahalia Jackson presented a concert of gospel music. With our final victory only days away, the eyes of the entire world focused on Montgomery.

At the Holt Street Baptist Church, site of the inaugural meeting just one year earlier, Dr. King addressed the opening session of the Institute:

> God still has a mysterious way to perform his wonders. It seems
> that God decided to use Montgomery as the proving ground for the
> struggle and triumph of freedom and justice in America. It is one of
> the ironies of our day that Montgomery, the Cradle of the Confed-
> eracy, is being transformed into Montgomery, the cradle of freedom
> and justice.

King not only praised the Negroes of Montgomery for their "wise
restraint and calm dignity," but he also commended the white community for their "discipline and moral sensitivity."

At this meeting we first heard Dr. King utter words that would be
echoed around the world a decade and a half later:

> Freedom must ring from every mountain side. Yes, let it ring from
> the snow-capped Rockies of Colorado, from the prodigious hilltops of
> New Hampshire . . . But not only that. Let Freedom ring from every
> mountain side—from every mole hill in Mississippi, from Stone Moun-
> tain of Georgia, from Lookout Mountain of Tennessee, yes, and from
> every hill and mountain of Alabama. From every mountain side let
> freedom ring.

The bells of freedom rang loudly just a few days later. On Monday,
December 17, 1956, the U.S. Supreme Court refused to reconsider its
decision in *Browder v. Gayle*. On Thursday, December 20, the order
arrived in Montgomery, prohibiting enforcement of bus segregation laws.
State and local laws were declared unconstitutional.

But the injunction applied only to Montgomery. Any broader application of the Supreme Court's decision required further legal action.
Negro leaders in other cities were already moving in that direction.

The December 20 *Alabama Journal* ran a front-page story under a
banner headline:

Bus Integration Ordered Here.

The Supreme Court order outlawing bus segregation arrived here today and an injunction against further enforcement of city and state laws in Montgomery went into effect immediately.

Most Montgomery Negroes were expected to wait until tomorrow to start riding city buses again after a year-long boycott, their leaders said. Two Negro mass meetings were called for tonight to make final plans.

The Rev. Martin Luther King, Jr., who has led the year-long boycott against segregated buses here, said, "in all probability" the Negroes will end their protest and start riding the buses tomorrow morning.

I missed both mass meetings that night, attending instead the training session of the Montgomery Council on Human Relations. The next day's *Journal* reported on our smaller meeting, under the front page headline: "Mixed Group Holds Meeting on Integration." In those days the very existence of an integrated group of people was front-page news. Reporter Joe Koenenn quoted at length from the MIA pamphlet we had distributed to potential bus riders at mass meetings. The pamphlet ended with:

If another person is being molested, do not arise to go to his defense, but pray for the oppressor and use moral and spiritual force to carry on the struggle for justice. According to your own ability and personality, do not be afraid to experiment with new and creative techniques for achieving reconciliation and social change. If you feel you cannot take it, walk for another week or two. We have confidence in our people.

At the same time, another pamphlet was circulating through the Negro community, this one obviously not from the MIA. With no indication of its source, the second leaflet encouraged Negroes to give up the boycott and get back on the buses. The writer argued that "there isn't a chance in the world of breaking segregation," while pointing out that Negro leaders were riding in "big cars" and "playing us for suckers." This tactic had been used several times before during the protest, so Negroes didn't take it seriously. They got a good laugh out of it.

On Friday, December 21, the *Montgomery Advertiser* reported on the previous night's mass meetings in the Negro churches:

> Rev. M. L. King, Jr., Negro leader of the boycott, brought some 1,200 applauding and happy Negroes to their feet with his call for a standing vote to return to the buses "on a nonsegregated basis."
>
> But King, who started the boycott in the same Holt Street Baptist Church one year ago, insisted that the return be one of absolute nonviolence.
>
> "If you can't take it, keep walking," King exhorted the group, the first of two to hear his message last night.
>
> "No one goes on that bus tomorrow alone," King told the frequently cheering crowd. "Every Negro bears on his shoulders the weight of responsibility of the 50,000 Negroes in Montgomery.
>
> "Violence must not come from any of us," he continued, "for if we become victimized with violent intents, we will have walked in vain."
>
> A second group of about 1,000 added their accord to the return to the buses a few moments later at the First Baptist Church at Ripley Street and Columbus Avenue.

Superintendent J. H. Bagley of Montgomery City Lines had announced earlier that his company would obey the law in seating the races. They had been losing thousands of dollars every day of the protest. Bus company officials were eager to get their struggling business back to normal.

Friday, December 21, 1956, exactly one year and sixteen days after the protest movement had begun, Negroes in Montgomery, Alabama, reboarded the buses. Reporters from both newspapers went out to ride the lines that once again traveled into Negro communities. Reporter Charles Sullivan's account appeared on the front page of the *Alabama Journal* that afternoon:

Early observation of Negroes riding the first integrated buses here reveal the absence of any open conflict between white and Negro passengers and the fact that many Negroes continue to sit in the rear of the buses.

Too, those Negroes taking seats near the front of the buss—those formerly reserved by custom for whites—appear in the main to be those riding "to prove their point" or to serve as examples to others of their race.

Those riding in the first few seats appear well-dressed and do not seem to be on their way to the type of job held by most Negro bus riders in Montgomery.

On Montgomery's first day of bus integration, a good many Negro riders forgot to pay and others had to be reminded to add a nickel to the dime they had already deposited. Fares before the boycott were only 10 cents here.

Sullivan's observations about some of the Negroes sitting in the front seats were accurate. Most ministers and other MIA leaders spent a good part of the day riding around, setting an example for other riders and watching for trouble. At the mass meetings the night before, ministers had been assigned to each bus route, especially during the morning and evening rush hours.

Another *Journal* reporter, Forrest Castleberry, rode with some of those leaders. His feature story in the same paper ran under the headline: "Mighty Good Ride."

"That was a mighty good ride."

"It was a great ride."

The comments came from the Rev. Ralph D. Abernathy and the Rev. Martin Luther King Jr., respectively, as they stood in Court Square just after completing their first ride on an integrated bus at 7:20 A.M. today.

The two top officials of the Montgomery Improvement Association boarded the South Jackson Street bus at Key Street and South Jackson. King took the third seat from the front and Abernathy sat in front of him on the second seat from the front.

A white minister sat beside King. He was the Reverend Glenn Smiley, a native of Texas who is now field secretary of the Fellowship of Reconciliation, with headquarters in New York City.

The ride into the heart of the city was without incident except for the flashing of bulbs by photographers, who had advance word as to when and where King and Abernathy would board the bus and got on at the same time they did.

King was the first to get on, and the driver asked: "Is this the reverend?"

"That's right," King answered. "How much?" referring to the fare. "Fifteen," said the driver. Answering questions from newsmen, King said this was the first time he had ridden a bus in more than a year— since December 1955, when the boycott started.

He construed the day's events as "very historical" and said he only hopes the movement (toward the end of Segregation) will continue to grow and "mean better human relations." Asked if he expected any trouble in Montgomery, King said he did not anticipate any major trouble. . . .

"If any trouble does occur I feel the proper authorities will take cognizance and that it will be stopped immediately," he said. He referred specifically to police and city officials.

Smiley said he took the ride just in order to get the reaction, as his organization had been urging nonviolence for forty-two years.

"This is the largest demonstration of this sort of thing in the United States and is tremendously interesting to us," he added.

Dr. King, himself, in *Stride toward Freedom,* described the amazingly friendly reaction he got when he boarded the first bus.

At 5:55 we walked toward the bus stop, the cameras shooting, the reporters bombarding us with questions. Soon the bus appeared; the door opened, and I stepped on. The bus driver greeted me with a cordial smile. As I put my fare in the box he said:

"I believe you are Reverend King, aren't you?"

I answered: "Yes I am."

"We are glad to have you this morning," he said.

I thanked him and took my seat, smiling now too.

My own reactions were much the same as I rode the buses that day. Though I had felt some apprehensions as I left for my first ride, drivers were friendly and courteous, and I witnessed no hostile actions by any riders, white or black.

I didn't have far to go to catch the bus that morning. The Cleveland Avenue bus stopped right in front of the church. As I left the house, Jeannie said, "If you see Glenn Smiley today, tell him to come over for dinner tonight."

I remembered to pass on Jeannie's invitation when I rode with Glenn on the last leg of my day's journey, catching the Cleveland Avenue bus one more time to head for home. That route passed by our house then made a big circle through the Negro neighborhood, passing by our house once again as it headed back downtown.

When I got off the bus, I ran to the house, eager to tell Jeannie what a wonderful day it had been. I have a reputation for telling long drawn-out stories, so it was not surprising that I was still standing on the front porch sharing my experiences with Jeannie when we heard a loud horn tooting. We turned to see the same bus from which I had just disembarked.

Having completed its swing through the neighborhood, the bus stopped in front of our house.

Glenn stood in its doorway. "What time is dinner?" he shouted.

"Make it 6:30," Jeannie called back.

"I'll be there," Glenn said, getting back into the bus.

The driver leaned over and smiled and waved as he closed the door and headed his bus toward town.

We were celebrating a victory. There was no doubt about that. It was a victory we had earned during the past year of struggles and trials. But we knew it was not just a victory for the Negroes of Montgomery. It was a victory for all of us.

# 9

# VIOLENCE

On that first historic day of integration, a group of young white men were standing at a downtown corner watching the buses roll by. "I never thought this would happen in Montgomery," one of them mused.

His friend responded, "The day's not over yet."

Those ominous words echoed the fears of many people in Montgomery, both white and black. There had been violence from time to time throughout the year-long protest, and almost everyone assumed that if the buses were integrated, the violence would escalate.

Whites recognized that bus integration would be only the first step. Furthermore, even the most peace-loving white people knew their own history. Violence, or the threat of it, had been used to maintain segregation for generations. No doubt it would be used again.

We in the MIA had our own concerns about violence. Shortly before our return to the buses, the Executive Board sent a letter to the city commission and the Montgomery police chief, asking for special police protection on dark streets, at the ends of bus lines, and in any other "danger zones." Our letter ended this way:

> We reaffirm our basic conviction that violence is both impractical and immoral. We have been training our people to remain nonviolent in word and deed, and not to return hate for hate. We believe that violence in our city will lead to a long and desolate night of bitterness, which will bring shame to generations yet unborn.

Not surprisingly, I was not aware of any direct response to our request, though the police were certainly on a higher state of alert. At the time of the Supreme Court's ruling in November, the revitalized Ku Klux Klan had called for a show of strength to keep Montgomery's Negroes "in their place." The *Alabama Journal* reported on November 14:

> A caravan of about 40 carloads of robed Ku Klux Klan members toured Negro residential areas of Montgomery last night, horns blowing, but police said they had no reports of violence.

A few minor incidents of vandalism had occurred even before we reboarded the buses. The cars of several of our leaders were damaged by acid thrown on them.

A much more serious pattern emerged on the buses themselves. When we began riding on an integrated basis, many Negroes chose to sit in back as before. But quite a few, including women, were brave enough to occupy seats in front. On several occasions a Negro woman sitting near the front of the bus would be followed off the bus by a white man, who would beat her with his fists, then jump into a car that had been following the bus.

We were glad we had held those training sessions. In each case the women held up their arms to protect themselves but never struck back. And those wonderful ladies became heroines as they reported their experiences at mass meetings. One woman said, "Shucks, I could have beat him up with one hand tied behind my back!" But people honored their commitment to nonviolence.

There was one incident, however, where that commitment was not upheld. A white man waited until a Negro woman took a seat in front of him on the bus. Then he left his seat, walked up to where the woman was sitting, and pulled out a wrench.

As he drew his arm back, ready to strike, another Negro woman decided she had to interfere. Rushing up to the man, she grabbed his arm, took the wrench from him, dragged him off the bus, and proceeded to beat him up!

Someone called the police, and both parties filed charges. When the cases went to court, remarkably, the white bus driver and many of the white passengers testified on behalf of the Negro woman! At the end of the trial, the white judge warned the white defendant to stay off the buses completely unless he could behave himself. The Negro woman was exonerated. A new day had come to Montgomery!

But within days, additional problems developed. City buses became targets as gunshots rang out all over town. One pregnant Negro woman was hit in both legs. Bullets narrowly missed several other passengers and drivers. As a result, the city commission canceled all bus runs after 5:00 P.M.

With this latest turn of events, however, came an outpouring of concern for bus drivers, who were in the greatest danger. And the Montgomery police department became more zealous to find the perpetrators of the violence.

Meanwhile, Jeannie and I had personal concerns on our minds. She was nearly full-term with our fourth child. Many parents in our situation might have been hoping for an early delivery, so the baby would be born before year's end, providing an additional income-tax deduction. We, however, didn't need that assistance. For many years, our salary was so low and our family so large, that we paid not a single cent in federal income tax.

So, even the newest member of our family made newspaper headlines. The *Montgomery Advertiser* ran a story on January 2, entitled: "5 Infants Welcomed to City with First Day of New Year." The last line of the article read: "St. Margaret's Hospital greeted baby No. 5, the fourth boy, at 12:43 P.M., the son of the Rev. and Mrs. Robert S. Graetz." David Ellis Graetz had arrived.

Five days later, on Sunday afternoon, I brought Jeannie and David home. My mother came down from Charleston, West Virginia, to help around the house for a while as she had done when Dianne was born. Mother roomed with eleven-month-old Dianne in the front bedroom. With two babies around, we were grateful for the extra help. The end of the protest considerably reduced the pressure on our family, but my schedule was still full.

The following Wednesday night, after tucking the children into bed and a short while later saying goodnight to Mother, we all retired for the night. At 2:00 A.M. came that explosion outside our house and Jeannie's exclamation, "My word! Another bomb!"

After making sure Mother and the children were all right and then assessing the damage, we visited with the friends and neighbors who came to check on us.

Standing outside the house in the darkness of that early morning, we heard the sounds of other bombs exploding. The attack had been very carefully planned. Rev. Ralph Abernathy was the prime target. Both his house and his church were bombed. The extensive damage to Bell Street and Mt. Olive Baptist churches caused the buildings to be condemned.

When Montgomery detectives broke the case a few weeks later, they were able to piece together the bombers' plans. That large unexploded bomb our friend had found in our yard was apparently the only one intended to be deadly. As the demolitions people from Maxwell Air Force Base told us, that bomb could have leveled the entire neighborhood, killing our whole family and many of our neighbors. God was indeed watching over us!

When the large bomb failed to work properly, the bombers circled back and threw a smaller one into the yard, hoping it would set off the first one. According to a list of potential targets found in the home of one of the bombers, that smaller bomb was intended for the home of Father Robert DuBose, a Negro Episcopal priest active in the protest.

I made this entry in the journal at Trinity Lutheran:

> Jan. 10, 2:00 A.M.—Parsonage bombed for the second time. Much more damage than first one. Larger bomb, made up of eleven sticks of dynamite and one piece of TNT found in driveway, failed to explode. Fuse had been lit, had gone out. "The hand of the Lord is not shortened." Four Negro churches and the parsonage of Rev. Ralph Abernathy were also bombed.

The *Montgomery Advertiser* published an extra edition that morning. Its headline story, of course, reported the bombings:

> At least five explosions rocked the early morning hours in Montgomery today as dynamite bombs were tossed at Negro residences and churches.
>
> Nobody was reported hurt from the series of blasts. . . .
>
> The first blast was heard by reporters at almost exactly 2 A.M. with the fourth reported shortly after 2:30 A.M. The intervening explosions came almost in clock-work precision.
>
> Reporters and photographers found the first at the home of the Rev. Bob Graetz, whose home was bombed in late August of last year, while he and his family were away from home.
>
> Today's bomb, while going off within five feet of the front door and smashing to door from its hinges, left Graetz, his wife, and two children unhurt. [The reporters couldn't keep track of our four children. Later in the article, we were up to three.]
>
> Another dynamite bomb, with 11 sticks of dynamite wrapped around a metal stick, was found lying in the driveway of the Graetz home.

The unexploded bomb presented quite a problem. Police experts feared it could still explode if it were bumped. They tried unsuccessfully to get a demolitions squad from Maxwell Air Force Base. Finally, two brave detectives, Charles Viunson and R. F. Houlton, volunteered to dispose of it. The *Advertiser* described the action:

> They clambered into a police car, Det. Houlton gingerly carrying the explosives on his lap to minimize jarring.
>
> The three [probably including Capt. E. P. Brown, the head detective] sped down Highway 31 during the early morning hours. North of the city near the river bridge the bundle was thrown in the Alabama River. [The television antenna had been removed earlier to check for fingerprints.]

The January 21 issue of *Time* magazine inaccurately reported our reaction:

> No one was injured, but Graetz and his family might well have been slaughtered as they ran from the house in panic; in their front yard police found still another bomb, made of eleven sticks of dynamite, which failed to explode because of a defective fuse.

At least they were good enough to carry the letter I wrote in response:

> Sir:
>
> Your Jan. 21 story on the second bombing of my home (along with another parsonage and four churches here) indicated that I and my family had fled in panic after the explosion. Nothing was farther from the truth. When the bomb went off, my wife sat up in bed and said, in a surprised voice, "My word! Another bomb!" Our two older children, aged 4 and 2 1/2, were rather excited, but not unduly disturbed. We thank God that he did not allow the larger bomb to explode; the police said it would have leveled the house. We can take the bombs and the nasty phone calls and letters; we can take the insults and the stares. But please, we don't want people to think we've started to get panicky and to run away. We have not moved, and we do not intend to.

In the meantime, our house was a mess! Besides the pieces of glass all over the newly varnished floor in the front room and tiny glass fragments peppering the drapes and the inside wall, plaster dust had settled on everything. The kitchen was a sea of litter. Every dish and glass, every pot and pan we owned had been propelled from its usual storage place. Most were broken. I later spent hours sorting through trash cans full of shards, trying to get a precise count of our loss for the insurance company.

Almost before the plaster dust had settled, Mrs. Rosa Parks was back in our kitchen, cleaning up debris for the second time. Several members of our church and other friends joined her.

Many of our white friends made a point of coming by to see us. When Mrs. Clara Rutledge visited, she not only brought us a wonderful beef roast, but she also sent her maid over to help us. Jeannie objected. Several people had already brought food. We didn't need more.

Mrs. Rutledge sat her down and gave her a motherly lecture. "Jeannie, a lot of us feel really bad about what has happened to you. We need to do something to help. Some of us are ashamed to be white right now. It is important that you let us do what we can. You just put that roast in your freezer and eat it later."

On the day of the bombing, Woody Draut passed along the information that our enemies were still intent on killing us. We should definitely not stay in our house overnight.

That is how our nighttime odysseys began. After friends helped us board up the windows and put in a temporary front door, Thursday evening we packed enough things for a week-long trip and loaded the seven of us into our car. That night we stayed with a Negro family, Dr. and Mrs. R. T. Adair.

As we prepared for bed, Dr. Adair noticed that I was still nervous and tense from all that had gone on, as well as from lack of sleep. He gave me some medication to calm me.

Within minutes I experienced a frightening reaction. My heart beat so hard I thought it would burst right out of my chest. How ironic, I thought. *The bombers couldn't kill me, but now I'm going to die here in the home of a friend just trying to help me.* The reaction subsided quickly, however, and soon we were all asleep.

Friday morning we made the trip back to our shattered house. And Friday evening we loaded up once again and drove to the home of Father Tom Thrasher, a white Episcopal priest, who had been a dear friend and a strong supporter. Tom, active in the Montgomery Council on Human Relations, spoke out strongly on racial issues.

The Thrashers lived in a beautiful home in an affluent section of Montgomery. Mayor Gayle lived right across the street. We wondered if the mayor ever found out we had been his neighbors for a night.

Saturday morning we headed home again. I made a couple of house calls that day and finished getting ready for Sunday school and church the next morning. That evening we got all packed up again, with a fresh stack of diapers for our two little ones, but when it was time to get into the car, Jeannie wouldn't move. "The rest of you can go if you want to," she said, "but I'm tired of running. I'm going to stay right here!" Mother and I concurred immediately. We were exhausted from our travels with four little children. That night we had the best sleep since before David was born.

We hadn't left the house because we were afraid. We only left because we had been told to. By now we felt much more horrid than frightened, yet we were still very much aware of that "circle of love" that continued to surround us.

That Sunday couldn't be like just any other Sunday, given the events of the previous week. The entry in the church log book reads:

> Jan. 13—Sermon theme today, "How Often Shall We Forgive?"
> Text: Matthew 18:21–35

Virtually every Negro minister in Montgomery preached about forgiveness that day, asking our congregations to forgive those who had perpetrated the violence. We were determined to maintain our nonviolence stance to keep reactions to the bombings under control. And we succeeded. Though people reacted in shock and anger, there was no violence.

A group of white business and professional men, the Men of Montgomery, also set a calm, rational tone after the bombings. They bought an ad in the *Advertiser* on January 11, that read:

> The problem facing us today is not a question of segregation or integration —
> It is violence!
> Those who are low enough to take it upon themselves to commit these dastardly acts can expect no sympathy from the citizens of Montgomery. We urge that no stone be left unturned to bring these cowards to justice and that they be punished to the fullest extent of the law.
> The responsible citizens of this community look to the officials

who are charged with maintaining law and order; namely, the Mayor and Commissioners, the Sheriff's office and the Judges of our courts to see that the guilty are caught and prosecuted.

Violence, by white or colored, cannot be tolerated. We call upon you who are causing this violence to realize you are accomplishing nothing but hatred, you are rapidly destroying our city. The tragic events of the last few weeks, if continued, will hurt you and your family.

THE FUTURE OF MONTGOMERY IS AT STAKE!!

The bombings, of course, caused a great deal of consternation and fear all over Montgomery. The police department called in all of their reserve forces and prepared for the worst. Bus service halted totally. The *Advertiser* reported, "Mayor W. A. Gayle may be considering a ban on all inter-racial gatherings such as sporting events . . . [The] commission urged a midnight curfew for all teen-agers in Montgomery."

Governor James Folsom offered a two thousand dollar reward for information that would help solve the case. City Commissioners later added another two thousand dollars.

The *Montgomery Advertiser* did some quick research and reported that because their targets were inhabited dwellings, those who had bombed the Abernathys' home and ours could receive the death penalty if convicted.

Public opinion was against the bombers. They had stepped across that invisible line that divided acceptable behavior from unacceptable behavior. The police department, too, was eager to solve the case. The crimes represented a signal to the Montgomery community that the official law enforcers couldn't keep the peace. Even rank-and-file police officers and detectives determined to set the record straight.

Within a week, three youngsters found a three-stick bomb hidden under a bridge. This "find" provided more clues for investigators, who found many similarities to the unexploded bomb at our home.

Two weeks later, about 4:30 on Sunday morning, the bombers struck again. The target this time was Dr. King's home. First reports were somewhat confusing. A small bomb had exploded about a block away between the (Negro) Peoples Service Station and Cab Stand and the home of a Negro family that had no connection with the protest leadership.

As police checked out the scene, they found another unexploded bomb on the Kings' porch—this one made of twelve sticks of dynamite. Only one of its two fuses had been lit. An expert, Assistant State Toxicologist Dr. Vann Pruitt rushed to the scene. In a delicate forty-five minute "operation," he removed the fuses and dismantled the bomb.

A watchman at the Kings' house reported walking out from the side of the house in time to surprise some white men in front. Apparently they had not quite finished their task. Hastily retreating, they threw something out of their car. Presumably, they were planning to set off the large bomb with the small one as they had attempted to do at our house. Once more they had failed.

The King family was in no danger, regardless of what had happened. Weeks before, they had been persuaded to move to a secret location.

Another key player reached the scene soon after the bomb exploded. City detective Jack Shows was off duty that Sunday morning, asleep at home about a mile away. Rushing to the area, he remained on the fringe of the crowd, looking at cars and license plates, searching for faces of suspects in the earlier bombings.

Shows's tactics paid off. He recognized a man named Henry Alexander and ordered Alexander followed. Less than eight hours later, in Selma, Alabama, about fifty miles away, police arrested Alexander. Partly because of the shock of his arrest and partly because the officers confronted him with considerable information about his involvement in the bombings, Alexander signed a confession, implicating several other white men. The police dragnet began picking up the other suspects, informing them that their co-conspirators had told of their involvement. These men confessed their own misdoings and began to inform on one another. Altogether seven white men were arrested.

Late one evening, the phone rang in our home. When I answered, the caller said, "Reverend, this is Captain Brown at the police department. We've arrested two men for throwing the bomb at your house that didn't go off. We'd like you to come down and sign a warrant against them."

Though the call seemed authentic, I had learned to be wary because of several previous attempts to trick me into meeting someone under strange, potentially dangerous circumstances. So I said, "Let me call you right back, to make sure this is really you."

When I phoned the police department, the Captain assured me that he had indeed called me. I drove downtown by myself in the dark, parking around the corner from the police station. Minutes later, I had signed warrants against Eugene Hall, forty-five, and Charley Bodiford, twenty-nine, charging them with attempting to bomb our house.

I turned to leave, but Captain Brown stopped me. "Reverend," he said, "since you came in, the street outside has filled with reporters. They've gotten word about the warrants. I figure you're probably tired of having your picture in the paper."

"You're right about that."

"Where is your car parked?"

When I told him, he explained how I could get to my car via some alleys without facing reporters.

I thanked him and left through the back door, certain I could trust him. Though the captain didn't like what I was doing or agree with my beliefs about race, his own code required him to treat me respectfully. I returned home without incident.

The seven arrested men were eventually released as their friends raised bail money for them one by one. These were not wealthy men, and the defense lawyers were reportedly charging a total of $50,000, an incredibly large sum in those days, to handle their cases. Soon an ad appeared in the paper:

NOTICE TO ALL WHITE PEOPLE
YOUR FINANCIAL
AID URGENTLY
NEEDED!
WANTED AT ONCE
100,000 CONTRIBUTORS
TO
LEGAL DEFENSE FUND
URGENT!

Police officials announced the bombers' connections with the local chapter of the Klan, and indeed the KKK mounted its own effort to raise money for their defense. By this time, however, public opinion had turned against both the Klan and the bombers; their fund-raising efforts scarcely reached outside their own membership.

When the cases against the seven alleged bombers were presented, the Montgomery County Grand Jury returned indictments against only four of them. Those whose charges involved bombs which had not exploded, including Hall and Bodiford, were freed.

On Monday, May 27, the trial of two of the alleged bombers began. On Thursday the trial ended. The prosecution presented conclusive evidence—confessions from both defendants, a picture of one of the two pointing out to police a place where they had stashed some unused dynamite, and handwritten notes found in their homes pertaining to their bombing targets.

The only defense argument stemmed from a justification of the system. In the defense attorneys' closing statements, they told the jury that a "not guilty" verdict would "sound a clarion call that 'you Negroes shall not pass'" and warned that "a guilty verdict will be a verdict for Martin Luther King and his imps who seek to destroy our Southern way of life."

The jury deliberated for one hour and thirty-five minutes before bringing in a verdict of *not guilty*. The defendants were free. The Klan had won.

At least they seemed to have won. But we had not counted on the intense emotional involvement of the local police. Their reputation as an effective law-enforcement body hinged on their solving the bombing case. The alleged bombers' acquittal was a slap in the face of the Montgomery Police Department.

In the weeks that followed, newspaper articles reported one or another of the seven being arrested, often for minor violations. Rumors floated back to us that others had lost their jobs or their homes, probably due to the outlandish attorney fees and unsuccessful Klan fund-raising activities.

Some time later, the father of one of the seven defendants killed himself by jumping from a downtown office-building window.

In the meantime, substantial sums of money poured in to rebuild the churches and homes that had been bombed. Still, rebuilding took considerable time. On May 18, 1958, I felt privileged to be the guest speaker at Bell Street Baptist Church when they moved into their new building.

By this time, we had planted a tree in the bomb crater in our front yard, even holding a little family ceremony there. We were determined to turn this scar of death into a visible symbol of life.

Insurance and gifts covered the loss of virtually all our personal property. But one particular gift meant more to us than anything else. Mrs. Gertrude Harris, who worked as a housemaid, earning two or three dollars a day, showed deep concern about what we had gone through. She went to her friends and neighbors, soliciting cash gifts in order to do something nice for us.

In a mass meeting at Maggie Street Baptist Church on Monday, April 29, 1957, when Mrs. Harris presented Jeannie with a new set of dishes and glasses, she said simply, "When they bombed the Graetzes, they bombed us."

Jeannie was so moved she could say little more than thank you. As for me, I felt this was the closest we had ever come to achieving my long-held dream of becoming accepted as Negroes. After that, we often told people, "When the bomb went off, it turned our skin dark."

But, of course, that dream could never totally be realized. As my wise friend counseled, we could never become Negroes, because we always had the option of leaving. And the time would come when we *would* leave—move away from Montgomery, and ultimately move away from Negro communities altogether. But for the time being, we were determined to stay as long as necessary to help our friends and neighbors achieve their goal of full equality.

# 10

## INTO THE FUTURE

Long before the buses of Montgomery were desegregated, the Montgomery Improvement Association began investigating other facets of racial discrimination and segregation. But we could not invest much energy in those activities until after the buses were truly integrated and the bombing confusion died down.

On March 7, 1957, the MIA Board appointed a Committee on the Overall Future Program of the MIA. I was one of fifteen members, including eight clergy and seven lay people, named to this panel. We met four times that month, but it took us about a year to hammer out a program for the future of Montgomery's Negro community.

In March, 1958, we presented to the MIA a ten-point program, setting up subcommittees for everything from political involvement and economic improvement to education and spiritual enrichment. I chaired the Community Relationships Committee, developing channels of interracial communication.

The Education Committee took steps immediately to move toward integration of Montgomery's public schools. Years passed before we reached that goal, but, notably, several Negro families had taken the incredibly bold step of sending their children to white schools in 1954 after the U.S. Supreme Court had ruled school segregation unconstitutional.

The Recreation Committee attempted to get the city to make more parks available to Negroes, hopefully by desegregating the present facilities.

Most active of all, and undergirding the work of the other nine committees, was the group focusing on civic and political education. Their primary function was to promote voter registration. Only as Negro people gained political power would we be able to accomplish our other goals. As yet only a handful of Negro citizens were allowed the privilege of voting. Mr. Rufus Lewis, who had done such an outstanding job heading up the Transportation Committee in the early days of the protest, now headed the Political Education Committee.

Long before we completed the task of putting together our ten-point program, I was given another major assignment. The MIA Board appointed me chairman of the Second Annual Institute on Nonviolence and Social Change, set for December 5–8, 1957. Related to our theme, "Freedom and Dignity Through Civic Responsibility," I called on my friend Paul Simon to address a plenary session and to conduct several seminars. A few weeks later, in a *Christian Century* article entitled "Montgomery Looks Forward," he wrote:

> Early in December, two years to the day after courageous Negroes started the successful bus boycott in Montgomery, Ala., I visited that city of bloodless struggle as the same people met for an appraisal they called the "Second Annual Institute on Nonviolence and Social Change." It was a quick glance back at victories attained and a confident look forward. Despite threats and active hostility on the part of much of the white community, the question was not *whether* they would go ahead but *where*.
>
> The institute's opening meeting was held in the Holt Street Baptist Church, the church where the Negro community had decided just two years before to stage the boycott.

Paul's article, filled with quotations from speakers at the Institute, also described two of his conversations with strangers as he headed for the airport to fly back to Illinois. In the first, Paul asked a young Alabama cattle farmer how he felt about school integration.

"It's coming," the young farmer replied. "It might be two or three years but it's coming."

Then Simon asked if he thought it might trigger more violence.

"Probably a little at first," the farmer replied, "but people will get adjusted to it. I served with 'em in the army and I got used to 'em."

The second stranger, Paul's cab driver and a former deputy sheriff, told Paul, "Integration is coming for sure. Don't get me wrong. I'm against it. But the orders have come down and that's it."

Asked about violence, the cab driver said some show-offs would make big claims, but "when they look down the gun-barrels of the President's troops, nothing is going to happen."

Paul concluded his article this way:

> If Martin Luther King and his friends have their way those show-offs, though they may put themselves in a spot where they have to "look down the gun-barrels of the President's troops," will also look into the hearts of people who hate injustice but "love their enemies."

Tensions still existed, and our people were still far from being totally liberated; but we had entered a period of relative calm, due largely to our reliance on love and nonviolence. Conflict cannot thrive if one party to that conflict will not fight back.

On January 25, 1958, a new development disturbed the relative calm in the Graetz household. I received an official call to become the pastor of St. Philips Lutheran Church in Columbus, Ohio. We did not want to leave, but we allowed God to direct us. About two weeks later I flew to Columbus to meet with Lutheran church officials and the church council at St. Philips. That night in my hotel room I felt confident that we were supposed to remain in Montgomery. A few days later I returned the call letter.

Jeannie and I "knew" we were going to live in Montgomery long enough to sink our roots down. The decision to stay pleased us because we had grown to love the South in spite of all of the turmoil. Also, at that time our congregation needed some intensive ministry.

Trinity Lutheran and the other congregations in Alabama were considering a transfer into the Lutheran Church—Missouri Synod. For me, even the thought of it was traumatic. I would have to appear before a Board of Colloquy, a group of ministers who would question me to determine whether my theology was acceptable to that church body. (After we left Montgomery, I was informed that some of the pastors who would have been on the board had already decided not to accept me. I was too controversial.)

Assuming we were going to stay in Montgomery, there was another problem we needed to deal with immediately. Margee would turn six the following November, and we had to arrange for her to start kindergarten in the fall.

But we had already found unacceptable the public grade school about a block and a half down Georgia Street. School buses filled with little children regularly slowed down as they made the turn from Cleveland Avenue to Georgia Street. If any of us were outside, the children would lean out of the bus windows and yell, "Nigger-lover, nigger-lover!"

Any public school in Montgomery would likely be just as bad; Margee could scarcely deny her identity as our daughter. The Holt Street Baptist Church, only a few blocks from our house, had a day school, however. So we called to enroll Margee, resolving that problem.

But after we moved to Columbus, we learned that the people at Holt Street had been forced to change their minds. By accepting Margee they would have lost their state subsidy because the school would then be integrated, still illegal in Alabama. And losing state support would have necessitated closing the school. Fortunately for all of us, we left Montgomery before they were forced to share that painful decision with us.

But leaving Montgomery was the farthest thing from our minds in the spring of 1958—until May 28, that is, when Ohio District president Ken Priebe and Pastor Dick Fenske came to Montgomery to discuss our proposed transfer to the Missouri Synod. On the way to the meeting at church, Pastor Priebe handed me a fat envelope, recognizable to all Lutheran pastors as a letter of call.

I was dismayed, having so recently been through this process. We had hoped we could count on staying in Montgomery for at least a little longer. To my further dismay I discovered that this was another call from St. Philips Lutheran in Columbus.

"Well," I said to Priebe, "I've already prayed about this. I'll hold the call for a while, so I won't seem to be acting too hastily. Then I'll send it back."

"You listen to me!" Pastor Priebe shot back. "Whose church is this, yours or the Lord's?"

"The Lord's," I answered, a little stunned.

"And who calls his men to where he wants them to be?"

"The Lord," I said.

"Then you let the Lord decide what you're supposed to do about that call!"

"Okay," I told him, feeling a little more confident now. "I'll pray about it and let the Lord decide. But I know what the answer is going to be."

The next day, before I had even taken time to pray, I sat down to write a letter to St. Philips Lutheran Church, feeling certain it was out of the question for us to consider moving anyplace before we had completed our negotiations with the Missouri Synod. I began the letter by explaining that we could not come in the immediate future, no matter what the ultimate answer might be.

By the time I had written those words, a silent but persistent voice kept saying to me, "Why not?"

I knew I needed to answer that question, but the longer I thought and prayed, the more I realized I had no answer.

After walking back across the lawn for lunch that day, I said to Jeannie, "I think the Lord wants us to go to Columbus."

Jeannie's reluctance to leave Montgomery proved even greater than mine. "You have to pray about it and decide what we're supposed to so," she said repeatedly over the next few days. "I'll accept whatever decision you make. But I don't want to go!"

My conviction that we should go to Columbus grew stronger each day. On Sunday, June 15, I announced to our congregation that I intended to accept the call to St. Philips. The members of Trinity voted to grant me my release.

Our move from Montgomery to Columbus was delayed, however. We seemed to have developed a pattern of having babies around the time of important events in our lives. On July 24 at 12:31 A.M., Kathryn Eileen Graetz was born, our fifth child and third daughter. We decided to wait until Kathy was a month old before we made the long trip.

It was a busy month. Besides all the work of packing, we took part in a furious round of farewell activities. The MIA arranged a special luncheon in our honor. In my comments that day, I said, "The only reason we feel comfortable about leaving now is that we know we are not running away under pressure. The one thing that would change that decision in a hurry would be another bombing."

Attorney Fred Gray, sitting beside me at the table, looked up and smiled, "I think that could be arranged," he joked. We all knew that nearly every time there had been a bombing or some other attack on the Negro community, white leaders had accused us of doing it ourselves.

When the Montgomery Council on Human Relations said goodbye, they presented us with a beautiful gift, a large, inscribed formica serving tray.

But we were also very moved when Martin and Coretta King took time out of their incredibly busy schedule to come by our house with their two children for a visit one evening. The Kings not only expressed their love, gratitude, and good wishes; they also brought us a farewell present, a *silver* serving tray. Those two trays from the Kings and the MCHR are among our most precious possessions and still find regular use in our household.

Martin had already written in our copy of *Stride toward Freedom,*

To my dear Friends: Bob and Jeannie Graetz

In appreciation for your genuine goodwill, your unswerving devotion to the principle of freedom and justice, and your willingness to suffer and sacrifice in order to make Montgomery's stride toward freedom a lasting inspiration. Martin

On Sunday, August 24, I preached my farewell sermon at Trinity Lutheran Church, and two days later the movers loaded our belongings for the trip north. A most important chapter in our lives had come to an end.

*The Graetz family in 1958. From left, Margee, Bobby, David, Bob, Jeannie, Kathy, Dianne.*

Months later, when some members from Trinity were visiting us in Columbus, they shared their mixed feelings about our departure. "None of us wanted you to leave," they told us. "But we knew that if you stayed, sooner or later you would be killed. So all of us accepted the fact that you had to leave."

They were probably right. In our naivete, we had grown complacent. Since we had seen no violence for a while, we had decided our troubles were over. But our members, who knew far better the depth of racial feelings in the South, sensed that the lull was nothing more than a period of calm before the next storm. And indeed, racial bigots snuffed out many lives during the years following our departure.

But once again God had intervened on our behalf. We could not know what was in our best interest, but he did. The same Lord who had directed our steps through all the years of preparation and had guided us through the period of turmoil in Montgomery, was now leading us into new fields of service, each with its own set of challenges and rewards, each with its own memories.

THESE HAVE been our memories of Montgomery, of Martin Luther King, and of all those wonderful people, black and white, who shared their lives and their love with us. Many of them, in addition to Martin, have since been called out of this life. But our memories of them will never die.

*Bob and Jeannie Graetz, 1998.*

# Index